**4 DIFFERENT BONUSES IN THIS BOOK**

# EOE DIET

## COOKBOOK

AN ELIMINATION DIET DESIGNED TO MANAGE EOE AND OTHER FOOD ALLERGIES WITH GLUTEN FREE , EGG-FREE , SOY-FREE AND NUT-FREE MEALS (6FED) . FEATURES RECIPES FOCUSED ON APPETIZERS , SIDE DISHES , BEVERAGES / SMOTHIES , KITCHEN STAPLES AND CONDIMENTS

BY SOPHIA J. CAMPBELL

1 | EOE DIET- The Six Food Elimination Diet.

# EOE (Eosinophilic Esophagitis) DIET COOKBOOK

An Elimination Diet Designed to Manage EOE and Other Food Allergies with Gluten-Free, Diary-Free, Egg-Free, Fish-Free, Soy-Free, and Nut-Free Meals (6FED). Features Recipes Focused on Appetizers, Side Dishes, Beverages/ Smoothies, Kitchen Staples and Condiments. 4 EXTRA BONUSES

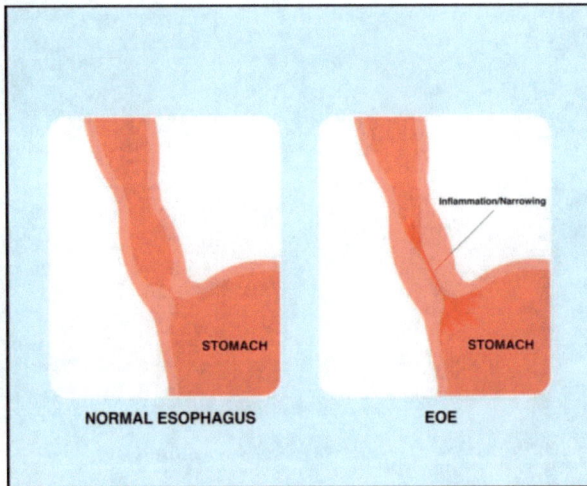

NORMAL ESOPHAGUS                    EOE

STOMACH                    Inflammation/Narrowing    STOMACH

## BOOK TWO OF THE SERIES: THE SIX FOOD ELIMINATION DIET FOR EOE

# HOW TO USE THIS COOKBOOK

Here's a simple guide in 5 easy steps on how to use this EOE Diet Cookbook effectively:

## 1. Understand Your Dietary Restrictions:

- Begin by familiarizing yourself with your specific dietary restrictions related to Eosinophilic Esophagitis (EOE) and other food allergies. Take note of the allergens you need to avoid, such as gluten, dairy, eggs, fish, soy, and nuts, as outlined in the 6FED approach.

## 2. Browse and Plan:

- Thoroughly explore the EOE Diet Cookbook. Take note of recipes that align with your dietary needs and preferences. Consider planning your meals for the week in advance to ensure a well-balanced and varied diet.

## 3. Prepare a Shopping List:

- Once you've selected the recipes you want to try, create a shopping list with all the necessary ingredients. Ensure that your pantry is stocked with essential items like gluten-free grains, dairy-free alternatives, egg substitutes, and allergen-free protein sources like poultry or meat.

## 4. Follow the Recipes Carefully:

- As you begin cooking, follow the cookbook's recipes meticulously. Pay attention to portion sizes, cooking times, and any specific instructions regarding allergen substitutes. The cookbook is designed to provide safe and delicious alternatives, so trust the process and enjoy experimenting with new flavors.

## 5. Monitor Your Body's Response:

- After incorporating meals from the EOE Diet Cookbook into your routine, pay close attention to your body's response. Note any changes in symptoms or how you feel overall. This step is crucial in determining the effectiveness of the cookbook in managing your EOE and food allergies. Consult with your healthcare provider if needed.

By following these five steps, you can make the most of your EOE Diet Cookbook, making meal planning and preparation a seamless and enjoyable part of managing your dietary requirements.

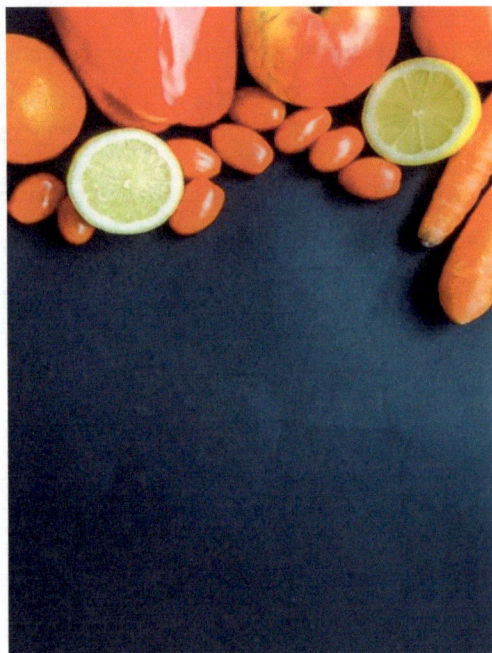

# ACKNOWLEDEMENTS

A Heartfelt thanks to my amazing husband, whose unwavering support fueled this cookbook's creation. Your encouragement and belief in my mission are my driving force. To my little inspiration, my 5-year-old daughter, your joy lights up my world. This cookbook is dedicated to you and all families facing Eosinophilic Esophagitis challenges.

A special shoutout to the resilient EOE community – your strength is truly inspiring. Big thanks to co-workers, friends, and family for understanding and accommodating my dietary needs. Your thoughtfulness during gatherings, picnics, and even Thanksgiving hasn't gone unnoticed. To my supportive friends and family throughout the writing process, your encouragement kept me going.

May this cookbook be a source of inspiration and support for those navigating the complexities of EOE and food allergies.

# TABLE OF CONTENTS

# INTRODUCTION

Welcome to a journey that promises not only to tantalize your taste buds but also to transform the way you approach managing Eosinophilic Esophagitis (EOE) and other food allergies. Are you tired of feeling restricted by your dietary limitations, longing for flavorful meals that cater to your health needs without sacrificing taste? Look no further – the EOE Diet Cookbook is here to revolutionize your culinary experience.

In a world where food can be both a source of pleasure and discomfort, we understand the challenges of navigating EOE and its dietary restrictions. That's why we've crafted this cookbook with you in mind, offering a diverse array of mouthwatering recipes that are not only safe for EOE but also free from gluten, dairy, eggs, fish, soy, and nuts – what we like to call the 6FED approach. This cookbook is more than just an assembly of recipes. It's a comprehensive guide designed to empower you in your journey towards better health. Our elimination diet is carefully crafted to help you identify trigger foods, while still enjoying a delicious and satisfying mealtime experience. Whether you're newly diagnosed with EOE or a seasoned veteran in the world of food allergies, you'll find something to delight your senses within these pages.

Dive into our collection of appetizers, side dishes, beverages/smoothies, kitchen staples, and condiments – each recipe thoughtfully curated to bring joy back to your kitchen. From savory snacks to indulgent treats, we've got you covered every step of the way. And as an added bonus, we've included four extra bonuses to enhance your culinary journey even further.

So, are you ready to embark on a culinary adventure that will leave you feeling nourished, satisfied, and empowered? Join us as we embrace the delicious possibilities of the EOE Diet Cookbook. Your taste buds as well as your health will eventually thank you. Let's get cooking!

# CHAPTER ONE: ALL ABOUT EOE

## What is EOE?

Eosinophilic Esophagitis (EOE) is a chronic immune-mediated disorder characterized by inflammation of the esophagus, the muscular tube that connects the throat to the stomach. In individuals with EOE, the immune system mistakenly identifies certain food proteins as harmful invaders, triggering an allergic response. This immune reaction leads to the accumulation of eosinophils, a type of white blood cell, in the esophageal tissue, causing inflammation and damage.

Common symptoms of EOE include difficulty swallowing (dysphagia), chest pain, food impaction, heartburn, and reflux. EOE can affect individuals of all ages, but it is more commonly diagnosed in children and young adults.

The exact cause of EOE is not fully understood, but it is believed to be related to a combination of genetic factors and environmental triggers. Diagnosis typically involves a combination of clinical evaluation, endoscopy, biopsy, and allergy testing.

Treatment for EOE often involves dietary management, medication, and lifestyle modifications. Elimination diets, which involve removing specific food triggers from the diet, are commonly used to manage EOE symptoms. Working closely with healthcare professionals, including allergists, gastroenterologists, and dietitians, is essential for effectively managing EOE and improving quality of life for individuals affected by this condition.

## The Six Elimination Diet

The Six Elimination Diet, often abbreviated as 6ED or 6FED, is a dietary approach aimed at managing conditions like Eosinophilic Esophagitis (EOE) and other food allergies. This diet focuses on eliminating six major allergen groups from the diet: gluten, dairy, eggs, fish, soy, and nuts. By removing these common allergens, the 6ED aims to reduce inflammation and alleviate symptoms associated with conditions like EOE. This approach is often recommended under the guidance of healthcare professionals, such as allergists or dietitians, who can help tailor the diet to individual needs and ensure proper nutritional balance.

While implementing the Six Elimination Diet, individuals are encouraged to consume a variety of whole, unprocessed foods that are naturally free from the eliminated allergens. This may include fruits, vegetables, lean proteins, and gluten-free grains. Additionally, alternative ingredients and cooking methods are often used to create flavorful and satisfying meals that comply with the diet's restrictions.

The Six Elimination Diet is not intended to be a long-term solution but rather a diagnostic tool to identify trigger foods and assess their impact on symptoms. Once trigger foods are identified, a personalized dietary plan can be developed to manage symptoms effectively while maintaining optimal nutrition and quality of life.

## Ingredients Substitutes Free from EOE Allergens

For individuals managing Eosinophilic Esophagitis (EOE) and adhering to an elimination diet free from common allergens like gluten, dairy, eggs, fish, soy, and nuts, finding suitable substitutes for these ingredients is key to enjoying a diverse and satisfying diet. Here are some ingredient substitutes that are free from EOE allergens:

1. **Gluten-Free Grains:** Replace wheat-based products with gluten-free alternatives such as rice, quinoa, millet, oats (certified gluten-free), sorghum, or buckwheat flour. These grains can be used in baking, cooking, and as a base for meals like stir-fries and salads.

2. **Dairy-Free Milk:** Go for dairy-free milk options like almond milk, coconut milk, rice milk, oat milk, or soy milk (if soy is tolerated). These plant-based milks can be used in recipes, smoothies, cereals, and beverages as a substitute for cow's milk.

3. Egg Replacements: Replace eggs in recipes with alternatives such as flaxseed or chia seed eggs,

mashed banana, applesauce, commercial egg replacers, or tofu. These substitutes can be used in baking, binding, and thickening recipes.

**4. Fish-Free Omega-3 Sources:** Incorporate plant-based sources of omega-3 fatty acids such as flaxseeds, chia seeds, hemp seeds, walnuts, and algae-based supplements. These ingredients can be added to smoothies, salads, baked goods, and savory dishes.

**5. Soy-Free Protein Sources:** Choose alternative protein sources free from soy, such as beans, lentils, peas, chickpeas, tofu (made from alternative ingredients like chickpeas or hemp), tempeh (made from alternative ingredients like black beans or quinoa), and seitan (wheat gluten).

**6. Nut-Free Flours and Butters:** Use flours made from seeds (e.g., sunflower seed flour, pumpkin seed flour) or legumes (e.g., chickpea flour, lentil flour) as nut-free alternatives in baking and cooking. For spreads and nut butters, consider options like sunflower seed butter, pumpkin seed butter, or tahini (sesame seed paste).

By incorporating these allergen-free substitutes into your recipes, you can create delicious and satisfying meals that comply with the dietary restrictions of EOE and other food allergies while still enjoying a diverse and nutritious diet. Always check labels for potential allergens and consult with a healthcare professional or dietitian for personalized guidance on ingredient substitutions and meal planning.

## Food Groups, Allergens and Labels

Navigating food groups, allergens, and labels is essential for individuals managing Eosinophilic Esophagitis (EOE) and other food allergies. Here's a breakdown to help you make informed choices:

### 1. Food Groups:

- **Grains:** Include gluten-free options such as rice, quinoa, millet, oats (certified gluten-free), sorghum, and buckwheat.

- **Proteins:** Choose lean proteins like poultry, beef, pork, lamb, and seafood (excluding fish if allergic). Plant-based options include beans, lentils, peas, tofu (if soy is tolerated), and tempeh.

- **Dairy:** Go for dairy-free alternatives such as almond milk, coconut milk, rice milk, oat milk, and soy milk (if soy is tolerated).

- **Fruits and Vegetables:** Enjoy a wide variety of fresh fruits and vegetables, focusing on seasonal and locally sourced options.

- **Fats and Oils:** Use heart-healthy fats like olive oil, avocado oil, coconut oil, and flaxseed oil in moderation.

- **Nuts and Seeds:** If not allergic, incorporate nuts and seeds such as almonds, walnuts, chia seeds, and flaxseeds into your diet for added nutrition.

## 2. Allergens:

- **Gluten:** Found in wheat, barley, rye, and their by-products.

- **Dairy:** Includes milk, cheese, yogurt, and butter derived from cow's milk.

- **Eggs:** Commonly used in baking, cooking, and as a binding agent.

**- Fish:** Includes all types of fish and fish-derived ingredients.

**- Soy:** Found in soybeans, soy products, and soy-derived ingredients.

**- Nuts:** Includes tree nuts (e.g., almonds, walnuts, cashews) and peanuts.

### 3. Labels:

**- Read Ingredients Lists:** Check product labels for potential allergens. Look for allergen statements indicating the presence of common allergens like gluten, dairy, eggs, fish, soy, and nuts.

**- Cross-Contamination:** Be aware of cross-contamination risks, especially in facilities that process allergens. Look for labels indicating if the product was processed in a facility that handles allergens.

**- Certifications:** Consider products with certifications like "gluten-free," "dairy-free," or "nut-free" for added assurance.

**- Contact Manufacturers:** If unsure about a product's ingredients or allergen status, reach out to the manufacturer for clarification.

By familiarizing yourself with food groups, allergens, and labels, you can make informed dietary choices that support your health and well-being while managing EOE and other food allergies. Always consult with a healthcare professional or dietitian for personalized guidance and recommendations tailored to your individual needs and preferences.

EGG
FREE

# CHAPTER TWO: APPETIZERS RECIPES

When managing Eosinophilic Esophagitis (EOE), finding appetizers that are both delicious and compliant with dietary restrictions can be a challenge. However, with a bit of creativity and careful planning, appetizers can become a delightful start to any meal without triggering EOE symptoms. In this section, we'll explore appetizer recipes tailored to the Six Food Elimination Diet, offering flavorful options that are free from gluten, dairy, eggs, fish, soy, and nuts. From savory bites to refreshing starters, these appetizers are designed to satisfy your taste buds while supporting your health goals. Let's dive into a world of appetizing possibilities!

## Baked Butter Beans with Basil and Garlic

**Cooking Time:** Approximately 25 minutes

**Nutritional Information (per serving - serves 4):**

- Calories: 250 kcal

- Protein: 8g

- Carbohydrates: 28g

- Fat: 12g

- Fiber: 6g

- Sodium: 300mg

## Ingredients:

- 2 cans (15 ounces each) butter beans, drained and rinsed

- 3 tablespoons olive oil

- 4 cloves garlic, minced

- 1/4 cup fresh basil leaves, chopped

- 1 tablespoon lemon juice

- Salt and pepper to taste

## Instructions:

1. Preheat your oven to 375°F (190°C). Grease a baking dish with olive oil lightly, or you could use a non-stick cooking spray.

2. In a large bowl, combine the drained and rinsed butter beans with olive oil, minced garlic, chopped basil leaves, lemon juice, salt, and pepper. Mix well to ensure the beans are

evenly coated with the seasonings.

3. Transfer the seasoned butter beans to the prepared baking dish, spreading them out in an even layer.

4. Bake in the preheated oven for 20-25 minutes, or until the beans are heated through and slightly crispy on the edges.

5. Once baked, remove the dish from the oven and let it cool for a few minutes before serving.

6. Garnish with additional fresh basil leaves if desired, and serve the baked butter beans warm as a delicious appetizer.

Enjoy these flavorful baked butter beans with basil and garlic as a nutritious and satisfying appetizer that's safe for individuals managing Eosinophilic Esophagitis (EOE) and adhering to the Six Food Elimination Diet.

## Roasted Red Pepper Hummus

**Cooking Time:** Approximately 35 minutes

**Nutritional Information (per serving - serves 6):**

- Calories: 120 kcal

- Protein: 4g

- Carbohydrates: 14g

- Fat: 6g

- Fiber: 3g

- Sodium: 180mg

## Ingredients:

- 1 can of drained and rinsed chickpeas (15 ounces)

- 2 large red bell peppers

- 3 tablespoons tahini

- 2 cloves garlic, minced

- 2 tablespoons lemon juice

- 2 tablespoons olive oil

- 1/2 teaspoon ground cumin

- Salt and pepper to taste

- Optional garnish: extra olive oil, paprika, chopped fresh parsley

## Instructions:

1. Preheat your oven to 400°F (200°C). Using a parchment paper, line a baking sheet.

2. Cut the red bell peppers in half and remove the seeds and membranes. On the prepared baking sheet, lace the pepper halves, cut side down.

3. Roast the red bell peppers in the preheated oven for 20-25 minutes, or until the skins are charred and blistered.

4. Remove the roasted peppers from the oven and let them cool slightly. Once cooled, peel off the charred skins and discard them.

5. In a food processor, combine the roasted red peppers, drained and rinsed chickpeas, tahini, minced garlic, lemon juice, olive oil, ground cumin, salt, and pepper.

6. Process the mixture until smooth and creamy, scraping down the sides of the food processor as needed.

7. Taste the hummus and adjust the seasoning, adding more salt, pepper, or lemon juice if desired.

8. Transfer the roasted red pepper hummus to a serving bowl. If desired, drizzle with extra olive oil and sprinkle with paprika and chopped fresh parsley for garnish.

9. Serve the roasted red pepper hummus with your favorite gluten-free crackers, sliced vegetables, or

as a spread on sandwiches and wraps.

Enjoy this flavorful and vibrant roasted red pepper hummus as a delicious appetizer or snack, perfect for individuals managing Eosinophilic Esophagitis (EOE) and adhering to the Six Food Elimination Diet.

## Moroccan Ground Recipes Kebobs

**Cooking Time:** Approximately 30 minutes

**Nutritional Information (per serving - serves 4):**

- Calories: 280 kcal

- Protein: 20g

- Carbohydrates: 10g

- Fat: 18g

- Fiber: 3g

- Sodium: 380mg

**Ingredients:**

- 1 lb ground beef

- 1 small onion, finely chopped

- 2 cloves garlic, minced

- 1/4 cup fresh parsley, chopped

- 2 tablespoons fresh cilantro, chopped

- 1 teaspoon ground cumin

- 1 teaspoon ground paprika

- 1/2 teaspoon ground cinnamon

- 1/4 teaspoon ground ginger

- 1/4 teaspoon ground turmeric

- 1/4 teaspoon ground black pepper

- 1/2 teaspoon salt, or to taste

- 1 tablespoon olive oil

- Wooden or metal skewers

**Instructions:**

1. If using wooden skewers, soak them in water for at least 30 minutes to prevent them from burning during cooking.

2. In a large bowl, combine the ground beef, chopped onion, minced garlic, parsley, cilantro, ground cumin, ground paprika, ground cinnamon, ground ginger, ground turmeric, ground black pepper, and salt. Mix well to thoroughly combine all the ingredients.

3. Divide the mixture into equal portions and shape each portion into a long,

sausage-like shape around the skewers, pressing firmly to ensure they hold together.

4. Preheat your grill or grill pan over medium-high heat. Using olive oil on all sides, brush on all sides.

5. Place the kebabs on the preheated grill or grill pan and cook for about 8-10 minutes, turning occasionally, until they are cooked through and slightly charred on the outside.

6. Once cooked, remove the kebabs from the grill and let them rest for a few minutes before serving.

7. Serve the Moroccan ground beef kebabs hot with your choice of sides, such as rice, couscous, or grilled vegetables.

Enjoy these flavorful Moroccan ground beef kebabs as a delicious and protein-packed dish, perfect for a weeknight dinner or entertaining guests. Adjust the seasonings according to your taste preferences, and feel free to customize the recipe with additional spices or herbs.

# Bacon Wrapped Chicken Meatballs

**Cooking Time:** Approximately 30 minutes

**Nutritional Information (per serving - serves 4):**

- Calories: 320 kcal

- Protein: 25g

- Carbohydrates: 2g

- Fat: 24g

- Fiber: 0g

- Sodium: 480mg

**Ingredients:**

- 1 lb ground chicken

- 8 slices bacon

- 2 cloves garlic, minced

- 2 tablespoons finely chopped fresh parsley

- 1/4 cup grated Parmesan cheese

- 1/4 cup almond flour or breadcrumbs (gluten-free if needed)

- 1/2 teaspoon dried oregano

- 1/2 teaspoon dried thyme

- 1/2 teaspoon smoked paprika

- 1/2 teaspoon salt

- 1/4 teaspoon black pepper

- Toothpicks

**Instructions:**

1. Preheat your oven to 400°F (200°C). Line a baking sheet with parchment paper.

2. In a large bowl, combine the ground chicken, minced garlic, chopped parsley, grated Parmesan cheese, almond flour or breadcrumbs, dried oregano, dried thyme, smoked paprika, salt, and black pepper. Mix until well combined.

3. Divide the chicken mixture into 16 equal portions and shape each portion into a small meatball.

4. Cut each bacon slice in half crosswise. Wrap each chicken meatball with a half slice of bacon and secure it with a toothpick.

5. Place the bacon-wrapped chicken meatballs on the prepared baking sheet, evenly spaced apart.

6. Bake in the preheated oven for 20-25 minutes, or until the bacon is crispy and the chicken is cooked through, with an internal temperature of 165°F (74°C).

7. Once cooked, remove the bacon-wrapped chicken meatballs from the

oven and let them cool for a few minutes before serving.

8. Serve the bacon-wrapped chicken meatballs hot as an appetizer or main dish, alongside your favorite dipping sauce or side dishes.

Enjoy these delicious bacon-wrapped chicken meatballs as a flavorful and protein-packed dish, perfect for parties, gatherings, or weeknight dinners.

## Baked Garlic Ginger Wings

**Cooking Time:** Approximately 40 minutes

**Nutritional Information (per serving - serves 4):**

- Calories: 320 kcal

- Protein: 25g

- Carbohydrates: 4g

- Fat: 22g

- Fiber: 1g

- Sodium: 680mg

## Ingredients:

- 2 lbs chicken wings, split at the joints, tips removed

- 2 tablespoons olive oil

- 4 cloves garlic, minced

- 1 tablespoon fresh ginger, grated

- 2 tablespoon Worcestershire sauce

- 1 tablespoon honey

- 1 teaspoon sesame oil

- 1/2 teaspoon red pepper flakes (optional)

- Salt and pepper to taste

- Chopped green onions and sesame seeds for garnish

## Instructions:

1. Preheat your oven to 400°F (200°C). Using parchment paper, line a baking sheet.

2. In a large bowl, combine the olive oil, minced garlic, grated ginger, Worcestershire sauce, honey, sesame oil, red pepper flakes (if using), salt, and pepper. Mix well to create the marinade.

3. Add the chicken wings to the bowl with the marinade and toss until they are evenly coated.

4. Arrange the marinated chicken wings in a single layer

on the prepared baking sheet.

5. Bake the wings in the preheated oven for 35-40 minutes, turning halfway through, or until they are golden brown and cooked through, with crispy skin.

6. Once cooked, remove the wings from the oven and let them cool for a few minutes.

7. Transfer the baked garlic ginger wings to a serving platter and garnish with chopped green onions and sesame seeds.

8. Serve the wings hot as a delicious appetizer or main dish, accompanied by your favorite dipping sauce or side dishes.

Enjoy these flavorful baked garlic ginger wings as a tasty and satisfying dish, perfect for sharing with family and friends.

## Indian Tempura Vegetable

**Cooking Time:** Approximately 40 minutes

**Nutritional Information (per serving - serves 4):**

- Calories: 320 kcal

- Protein: 25g

- Carbohydrates: 4g

- Fat: 22g

- Fiber: 1g

- Sodium: 680mg

## Ingredients:

- 2 lbs chicken wings, split at the joints, tips removed

- 2 tablespoons olive oil

- 4 cloves garlic, minced

- 1 tablespoon fresh ginger, grated

- 2 tablespoons Worcestershire sauce

- 1 tablespoon honey

- 1 teaspoon sesame oil

- 1/2 teaspoon red pepper flakes (optional)

- Salt and pepper to taste

- Chopped green onions and sesame seeds for garnish

## Instructions:

1. Preheat your oven to 400°F (200°C). Line the baking sheet using a parchment paper.

2. In a large bowl, combine the olive oil, minced garlic, grated ginger, Worcestershire sauce, honey, sesame oil, red pepper flakes (if using), salt, and pepper. Mix well to create the marinade.

3. Add the chicken wings to the bowl with the marinade and toss until they are evenly coated.

4. Arrange the marinated chicken wings in a single layer on the prepared baking sheet.

5. Bake the wings in the preheated oven for 35-40 minutes, turning halfway through, or until they are golden brown and cooked through, with crispy skin.

6. Once cooked, remove the wings from the oven and let them cool for a few minutes.

7. Transfer the baked garlic ginger wings to a serving platter and garnish with chopped green onions and sesame seeds.

8. Serve the wings hot as a delicious appetizer or main dish, accompanied by your favorite dipping sauce or side dishes.

Enjoy these flavorful baked garlic ginger wings as a tasty and satisfying dish, perfect for sharing with family and friends. Adjust the seasonings according to your taste preferences, and feel free to customize the recipe with additional herbs or spices.

## Herbed Hummus

**Cooking Time:** Approximately 15 minutes

**Nutritional Information (per serving - serves 6):**

- Calories: 140 kcal

- Protein: 5g

- Carbohydrates: 13g

- Fat: 8g

- Fiber: 4g

- Sodium: 220mg

**Ingredients:**

- 1 can of drained and rinsed 15 ounces of chickpeas

- 2 tablespoons tahini

- 2 cloves garlic, minced

- 2 tablespoons lemon juice

- 2 tablespoons olive oil

- 1/4 cup fresh parsley, chopped

- 2 tablespoons fresh cilantro, chopped

- 1 tablespoon fresh dill, chopped

- Salt and pepper to taste

- Optional garnish: extra olive oil, paprika, chopped fresh herbs

**Instructions:**

1. In a food processor, combine the drained and rinsed chickpeas, tahini, minced garlic, lemon juice, olive oil, chopped parsley, chopped cilantro, and chopped dill.

2. Process the mixture until smooth and creamy, scraping down the sides of the food processor as needed.

3. Taste the hummus and adjust the seasoning, adding more salt, pepper, or lemon juice if desired.

4. Transfer the herbed hummus to a serving bowl. If desired, drizzle with extra olive oil and sprinkle with paprika and chopped fresh herbs for garnish.

5. Serve the herbed hummus with your favorite gluten-free crackers, sliced vegetables, or as a spread on sandwiches and wraps.

Enjoy this flavorful and vibrant herbed hummus as a delicious appetizer or snack, perfect for individuals managing Eosinophilic Esophagitis (EOE) and adhering to the Six Food Elimination Diet. Adjust the seasonings according to your taste preferences, and feel free to customize the recipe with additional herbs or spices.

## Pico De Gauo

**Cooking Time:** Approximately 20 minutes

**Nutritional Information (per serving - serves 6):**

- Calories: 30 kcal

- Protein: 1g

- Carbohydrates: 7g

- Fat: 0g

- Fiber: 2g

- Sodium: 5mg

**Ingredients:**

- 4 ripe tomatoes, diced

- 1/2 small red onion, finely chopped

- 1 seeded and finely chopped jalapeño pepper,

- 1/4 cup fresh cilantro, chopped

- 1 tablespoon fresh lime juice

- 1/2 teaspoon ground cumin

- Salt and pepper to taste

## Instructions:

1. In a medium bowl, combine the diced tomatoes, chopped red onion, chopped jalapeño pepper, chopped cilantro, lime juice, and ground cumin.

2. To combine all the ingredients, mix well.

3. Season the pico de gallo with salt and pepper to taste.

4. Refrigerate for at least 30 minutes to allow the flavors to meld together, after covering the bowl with a plastic wrap.

5. Once chilled, remove the pico de gallo from the refrigerator and give it a final stir.

6. Serve the pico de gallo as a topping for tacos, nachos, or grilled meats, or as a dip with tortilla chips.

Enjoy this fresh and flavorful pico de gallo as a delicious

accompaniment to your favorite Mexican-inspired dishes. Adjust the seasonings according to your taste preferences, and feel free to customize the recipe with additional ingredients like diced avocado, corn, or black beans.

## Olive Tapenade

**Cooking Time:** Approximately 15 minutes

**Nutritional Information (per serving - serves 6):**

- Calories: 90 kcal

- Protein: 0g

- Carbohydrates: 3g

- Fat: 10g

- Fiber: 1g

- Sodium: 220mg

**Ingredients:**

- 1 cup pitted black olives

- 1/4 cup pitted green olives

- 2 cloves garlic, minced

- 1 tablespoon capers, drained

- 2 tablespoons fresh parsley, chopped

- 1 tablespoon fresh lemon juice

- 1 teaspoon Dijon mustard

- 2 tablespoons olive oil

- Salt and pepper to taste

**Instructions:**

1. In a food processor, combine the pitted black olives, pitted green olives, minced garlic, drained capers, chopped parsley, lemon juice, and Dijon mustard.

2. Pulse the mixture until it is coarsely chopped and well combined, but still has some texture.

3. With the food processor running, gradually add the olive oil in a steady stream until the tapenade reaches your desired consistency.

4. Taste the tapenade and adjust the seasoning, adding more salt, pepper, or lemon juice if desired.

5. Transfer the olive tapenade to a serving bowl.

6. Serve the olive tapenade as a spread on bread or crackers, or as a topping for grilled meats or fish.

Enjoy this flavorful and versatile olive

tapenade as a delicious addition to your appetizer spread or as a condiment for various dishes. Adjust the seasonings according to your taste preferences, and feel free to customize the recipe with additional ingredients like anchovies, sun-dried tomatoes, or fresh herbs.

## Roasted Cherry Tomatoes

**Cooking Time:** Approximately 25 minutes

**Nutritional Information (per serving - serves 4):**

- Calories: 60 kcal

- Protein: 2g

- Carbohydrates: 6g

- Fat: 4g

- Fiber: 1g

- Sodium: 220mg

**Ingredients:**

- 2 cups cherry tomatoes, halved

- 2 cloves garlic, minced

- 2 tablespoons olive oil

- 1 tablespoon fresh thyme leaves

- 1/2 teaspoon dried oregano

- Salt and pepper to taste

## Instructions:

1. Preheat your oven to 400°F (200°C). Line a baking sheet using a parchment paper.

2. In a large bowl, combine the halved cherry tomatoes, minced garlic, olive oil, fresh thyme leaves, dried oregano, salt, and pepper. Toss until the tomatoes are evenly coated with the seasoning.

3. Spread the seasoned cherry tomatoes in a single layer on the prepared baking sheet.

4. Roast the cherry tomatoes in the preheated oven for 20-25 minutes, or until they are soft and slightly caramelized.

5. Once roasted, remove the cherry tomatoes from the oven and let them cool for a few minutes before serving

6. Serve the roasted cherry tomatoes as a side dish or use them as a topping for salads, pasta, or grilled meats.

Enjoy these flavorful and vibrant roasted cherry tomatoes as a delicious and versatile addition to your meals. Adjust the seasoning according to your taste preferences, and feel free to customize the recipe with additional herbs or spices.

## Smashed Potatoes

**Cooking Time:** Approximately 35 minutes

**Nutritional Information (per serving - serves 4):**

- Calories: 150 kcal

- Protein: 2g

- Carbohydrates: 20g

- Fat: 7g

- Fiber: 2g

- Sodium: 220mg

**Ingredients:**

- 1 lb baby potatoes

- 2 tablespoons olive oil

- 2 cloves garlic, minced

- 1 tablespoon fresh rosemary, chopped

- Salt and pepper to taste

**Instructions:**

1. Preheat your oven to 400°F (200°C). Line a baking sheet using a parchment paper.

2. Placing the baby potatoes into a large pot, cover them using water. Bring the water to a boil and cook the potatoes for 15-20 minutes, or until they are fork-tender.

3. Drain the cooked potatoes and let them cool slightly.

4. On the prepared baking sheet, use a fork or potato masher to gently smash each potato, flattening it slightly but keeping it intact.

5. In a small bowl, combine the olive oil, minced garlic, chopped rosemary, salt, and pepper.

6. Brush the seasoned olive oil mixture over the smashed potatoes, making sure to coat each potato evenly.

7. Roast the smashed potatoes in the preheated oven for 15-20 minutes, or until they are crispy and golden brown.

8. Once roasted, remove the smashed potatoes from the oven and let them cool for a few minutes before serving.

9. Serve the smashed potatoes as a side dish or use them as a base for toppings like sour cream, cheese, or bacon.

Enjoy these flavorful and crispy smashed potatoes as a delicious and versatile addition to your meals. Adjust the seasoning according to your taste preferences, and feel free to customize the recipe with additional herbs or spices.

## Pulled Pork Lettuce Tacos

**Cooking Time:** Approximately 8 hours (slow cooker) or 3-4 hours (oven)

**Nutritional Information (per serving - serves 4):**

- Calories: 320 kcal

- Protein: 30g

- Carbohydrates: 5g

- Fat: 20g

- Fiber: 1g

- Sodium: 200mg

## Ingredients:

- 2 lbs pork shoulder or pork butt, trimmed of excess fat

- 1 small onion, finely chopped

- 4 cloves garlic, minced

- 1 teaspoon ground cumin

- 1 teaspoon chili powder

- 1 teaspoon smoked paprika

- 1/2 teaspoon ground coriander

- 1/2 teaspoon ground cinnamon

- 1/2 teaspoon ground cayenne pepper (optional)

- Salt and pepper to taste

- 1/2 cup chicken or vegetable broth

- 1 head iceberg lettuce, leaves separated

- Optional toppings: diced tomatoes, diced red onion, sliced avocado, chopped cilantro, lime wedges

## Instructions:

1. In a small bowl, combine the ground cumin, chili powder, smoked paprika, ground coriander, ground cinnamon, ground cayenne pepper (if using), salt, and pepper. To create a spice rub, mix well.

2. Rub the spice mixture all over the trimmed pork

shoulder or pork butt, ensuring it is evenly coated.

3. Place the pork in a slow cooker or roasting pan. Add the chopped onion and minced garlic around the pork.

4. Pour the chicken or vegetable broth over the pork.

5. If using a slow cooker, cover and cook on low for 8 hours or on high for 4 hours, or until the pork is tender and easily shreds with a fork.

6. If using an oven, preheat your oven to 325°F (160°C). Cover the roasting pan with foil and roast the pork for 3-4 hours, or until the pork is tender and easily shreds with a fork.

7. Once cooked, remove the pork from the slow cooker or roasting pan and shred it using two forks.

8. To assemble the lettuce tacos, place a spoonful of the shredded pork in each lettuce leaf. Top with diced tomatoes, diced red onion, sliced avocado, chopped cilantro, and a squeeze of lime juice, if desired.

9. Serve the pulled pork lettuce tacos immediately, and enjoy!

Enjoy these delicious and flavorful pulled

pork lettuce tacos as a satisfying and nutritious meal. Adjust the seasoning according to your taste preferences, and feel free to customize the recipe with additional toppings or condiments.

# CHAPTER FOUR: SIDE DISHES RECIPES

Side dishes are an essential component of any meal, adding variety, texture, and flavor to the dining experience. For individuals managing Eosinophilic Esophagitis (EOE), side dishes play an even more critical role, as they provide an opportunity to include a diverse range of safe and allergen-free ingredients. In this section of the EOE Diet Cookbook, we explore a collection of side dish recipes tailored to the Six Food Elimination Diet. These recipes are designed to be free from gluten, dairy, eggs, fish, soy, and nuts, offering flavorful and nutritious options that align with the dietary needs of EOE patients. From vibrant salads to comforting vegetable dishes, these side dishes are sure to complement any main course while supporting your health goals. Let's embark on a journey of culinary creativity and nourishment with these side dish recipes!

## Mexican Pink Beans and Rice

**Cooking Time:** Approximately 45 minutes

**Nutritional Information (per serving - serves 4):**

- Calories: 330 kcal

- Protein: 15g

- Carbohydrates: 60g

- Fat: 2g

- Fiber: 15g

- Sodium: 520mg

**Ingredients:**

- 1 cup pink beans, soaked overnight and drained

- 1 cup long-grain white rice

- 1 small onion, finely chopped

- 1 clove garlic, minced

- 1 seeded and finely chopped jalapeño pepper

- 1 teaspoon ground cumin

- 1 teaspoon chili powder

- 1/2 teaspoon smoked paprika

- 1/2 teaspoon ground coriander

- 1/2 teaspoon dried oregano

- 1/4 teaspoon ground cinnamon

- 1/4 teaspoon ground cayenne pepper (optional)

- 2 cups vegetable broth

- Salt and pepper to taste

- Fresh cilantro leaves for garnish

**Instructions:**

1. Over medium heat, in a large pot, heat a tablespoon of olive oil. Add your already chopped onion and the minced garlic, and you should sauté for about 2-3 minutes, or until the onion is soft and translucent.

2. Add the chopped jalapeño pepper, ground cumin, chili powder, smoked paprika, ground coriander, dried oregano, ground cinnamon, and ground cayenne pepper (if using). Stir well to coat the onion as well as the garlic together with the spices.

3. Add the soaked and drained pink beans to the pot, along with the long-grain white rice. Stir to combine.

4. Pour the vegetable broth into the pot, making sure it covers the beans and rice by about an inch. Bring the mixture to a boil, then reduce the heat to low, cover the pot, and simmer for 20-25 minutes, or until the beans and rice are cooked through and tender.

5. Once cooked, remove the pot from

the heat and let it sit, covered, for 5 minutes to allow the flavors to meld together.

6. Taste the Mexican pink beans and rice and adjust the seasoning, adding more salt, pepper, or spices if desired.

7. Serve this dish hot and garnish with fresh cilantro leaves.

Enjoy this flavorful and satisfying Mexican pink beans and rice dish as a delicious main course or side dish. Adjust the seasoning according to your taste preferences, and feel free to customize the recipe with additional ingredients like diced tomatoes, bell peppers, or corn.

## Cabbage and Fennel Slaw

**Cooking Time:** Approximately 15 minutes

**Nutritional Information (per serving - serves 4):**

- Calories: 70 kcal

- Protein: 1g

- Carbohydrates: 6g

- Fat: 5g

- Fiber: 2g

- Sodium: 210mg

## Ingredients:

- 1/2 small cabbage, thinly sliced

- 1 small fennel bulb, thinly sliced

- 1/4 cup mayonnaise (gluten-free if needed)

- 1 tablespoon apple cider vinegar

- 1 teaspoon honey

- 1 teaspoon Dijon mustard

- 1/4 teaspoon celery seed (optional)

- Salt and pepper to taste

- Chopped fresh parsley for garnish

## Instructions:

1. In a large bowl, combine the thinly sliced cabbage and fennel.

2. In a small bowl, whisk together the mayonnaise, apple cider vinegar, honey, Dijon mustard, and celery seed (if using).

3. Pour the dressing over the cabbage and fennel, and toss until the vegetables are evenly coated.

4. With salt and pepper, season the slaw to taste.

5. With the aid of a plastic wrap, cover the

bowl and refrigerate it for at least 30 minutes to allow the flavors to meld together.

6. Once chilled, remove the slaw from the refrigerator and give it a final stir.

7. Serve the cabbage and fennel slaw cold, garnished with chopped fresh parsley.

Enjoy this refreshing and crunchy cabbage and fennel slaw as a delicious side dish or topping for sandwiches and wraps. Adjust the seasoning according to your taste preferences, and feel free to customize the recipe with additional ingredients like shredded carrots, red onion, or bell peppers.

## Brown Rice and Mushroom Pilaf

**Cooking Time:** Approximately 40 minutes

**Nutritional Information (per serving - serves 4):**

- Calories: 220 kcal

- Protein: 5g

- Carbohydrates: 40g

- Fat: 5g

- Fiber: 3g

- Sodium: 160mg

## Ingredients:

- 1 cup brown rice, rinsed and drained

- 2 cups vegetable broth

- 2 tablespoons olive oil

- 1 small onion, finely chopped

- 2 cloves garlic, minced

- 8 ounces cremini mushrooms, sliced

- 1/2 teaspoon dried thyme

- 1/2 teaspoon dried rosemary

- Salt and pepper to taste

- Chopped fresh parsley for garnish

## Instructions:

1. In a medium pot, combine the brown rice and vegetable broth. Bring the mixture to a boil, then reduce the heat to low, cover the pot, and simmer for 35-40 minutes, or until the rice is tender and the liquid is absorbed.

2. While the rice is cooking, heat the olive oil in a large skillet over medium heat. Add your already chopped onion and the minced garlic, and you

sauté for about 2-3 minutes, or until the onion is soft and translucent.

3. Add the sliced cremini mushrooms to the skillet, along with the dried thyme and dried rosemary. Next, sauté for about 5-7 minutes, or until you notice the mushrooms are golden brown and tender.

4. Once the rice is cooked, add it to the skillet with the mushrooms. Stir well to combine all the ingredients.

5. Season the brown rice and mushroom pilaf with salt and pepper to taste.

6. Garnish the pilaf with chopped fresh parsley before serving.

7. Serve the brown rice and mushroom pilaf hot as a delicious side dish or main course.

Enjoy this hearty and flavorful brown rice and mushroom pilaf as a nutritious and satisfying addition to your meals. Adjust the seasoning according to your taste preferences, and feel free to customize the recipe with additional ingredients like diced bell peppers or carrots.

# Italian Red Cabbage Salad

**Cooking Time:** Approximately 15 minutes

**Nutritional Information (per serving - serves 4):**

- Calories: 140 kcal

- Protein: 2g

- Carbohydrates: 10g

- Fat: 10g

- Fiber: 3g

- Sodium: 220mg

**Ingredients:**

- 1 thinly sliced small head red cabbage

- 1/4 cup extra-virgin olive oil

- 2 tablespoons red wine vinegar

- 1 tablespoon Dijon mustard

- 1 clove garlic, minced

- 1/2 teaspoon dried oregano

- 1/2 teaspoon dried basil

- Salt and pepper to taste

- Grated Parmesan cheese for garnish

- Chopped fresh parsley for garnish

## Instructions:

1. Into a large bowl, you combine all the thinly sliced red cabbage.

2. In a small bowl, whisk together the extra-virgin olive oil, red wine vinegar, Dijon mustard, minced garlic, dried oregano, and dried basil.

3. Pour the dressing over the red cabbage and toss until the cabbage is evenly coated.

4. Season the Italian red cabbage salad with salt and pepper to taste.

5. Cover the bowl using a plastic wrap and you refrigerate it for at least 30 minutes to allow the flavors to meld together properly.

6. Once chilled, remove the Italian red cabbage salad from the refrigerator and give it a final stir.

7. Serve the salad cold, garnished with grated Parmesan cheese and chopped fresh parsley.

Enjoy this vibrant and flavorful Italian red cabbage salad as a refreshing side dish or topping for sandwiches and wraps. Adjust the seasoning according to your taste preferences, and feel free to customize the recipe with additional ingredients like sliced red onion, cherry tomatoes, or Kalamata olives.

## Romaine and Cilantro Salad with Lime-Olive Oil Dressings

**Cooking Time:** Approximately 10 minutes

**Nutritional Information (per serving - serves 4):**

- Calories: 150 kcal

- Protein: 3g

- Carbohydrates: 6g

- Fat: 14g

- Fiber: 2g

- Sodium: 230mg

**Ingredients:**

- 1 head romaine lettuce, chopped

- 1/2 cup fresh cilantro leaves, chopped

- 1/4 cup extra-virgin olive oil

- 2 tablespoons fresh lime juice

- 1 teaspoon honey

- 1/4 teaspoon ground cumin

- Salt and pepper to taste

- Optional garnish: sliced avocado, cherry tomatoes, red onion

## Instructions

1. In a large bowl, combine the chopped romaine lettuce and chopped cilantro leaves.

2. In a small bowl, whisk together the extra-virgin olive oil, fresh lime juice, honey, ground cumin, salt, and pepper.

3. Pour the lime-olive oil dressing over the romaine and cilantro, and toss until the greens are evenly coated.

4. Season the salad with additional salt and pepper to taste.

5. If desired, garnish the salad with sliced avocado, cherry tomatoes, or red onion.

6. Serve the romaine and cilantro salad immediately.

Enjoy this vibrant and refreshing romaine and cilantro salad with lime-olive oil dressing as a delicious side dish or light meal. Adjust the seasoning according to your taste preferences, and feel free to customize the recipe with additional ingredients like diced bell peppers, black beans, or corn.

## Chickpea Dinner Rolls (Yeast Free-Grain Free Salad)

**Cooking Time:** Approximately 25 minutes

**Nutritional Information (per serving - serves 4):**

- Calories: 220 kcal

- Protein: 9g

- Carbohydrates: 30g

- Fat: 7g

- Fiber: 6g

- Sodium: 340mg

**Ingredients:**

- 1 can of drained and rinsed 15 ounces of chickpeas

- 3 tablespoons olive oil

- 2 tablespoons water

- 2 tablespoons honey

- 1/2 teaspoon baking powder

- 1/4 teaspoon salt

- Optional: sesame seeds, poppy seeds, or dried herbs for topping

**Instructions:**

1. Preheat your oven to 350°F (175°C). Line a baking sheet using a parchment paper.

2. In a food processor, combine the drained and rinsed chickpeas, olive oil, water, honey, baking powder, and salt.

3. Process the mixture until it forms a smooth dough.

4. Divide the dough into 4 equal portions and shape each portion into a ball.

5. Place the balls of dough on the prepared baking sheet, evenly spaced apart.

6. If desired, sprinkle the tops of the dough balls with sesame seeds, poppy seeds, or dried herbs for added flavor and texture.

7. Bake the chickpea dinner rolls in the preheated oven for 20-25 minutes, or until they are golden brown and cooked through.

8. Once baked, remove the chickpea dinner rolls from the oven and let them cool for a few minutes before serving.

9. Serve the chickpea dinner rolls warm as a delicious and grain-free alternative to traditional dinner rolls.

Enjoy these flavorful and nutritious chickpea dinner rolls as a satisfying and protein-packed addition to your meals. Adjust the seasoning according to your taste preferences, and feel free to customize the recipe with additional ingredients like garlic powder, onion powder, or dried herbs.

## Thai Coconut Vegetable Soup

**Cooking Time:** Approximately 30 minutes

**Nutritional Information (per serving - serves 4):**

- Calories: 220 kcal

- Protein: 5g

- Carbohydrates: 14g

- Fat: 17g

- Fiber: 3g

- Sodium: 540mg

## Ingredients:

- 1 tablespoon coconut oil

- 1 small onion, finely chopped

- 2 cloves garlic, minced

- 1 tablespoon fresh ginger, grated

- 1 red bell pepper, thinly sliced

- 1 small zucchini, thinly sliced

- 1 small carrot, thinly sliced

- 1 tablespoon Thai red curry paste

- 1 can (14 ounces) coconut milk

- 3 cups vegetable broth

- 2 tablespoons soy sauce (gluten-free if needed)

- 1 tablespoon lime juice

- 1 teaspoon honey

- Salt and pepper to taste

- This is completely optional, garnish with chopped fresh cilantro and lime wedges

## Instructions:

1. Heat the coconut oil over medium heat, in a large pot. Add the chopped onion, minced garlic, and grated ginger, and sauté for 2-3 minutes, or until the onion is soft and translucent.

2. Add the thinly sliced red bell pepper, zucchini, and carrot to the pot. Sauté for an additional 3-4 minutes, or until the vegetables are slightly tender.

3. Stir in the Thai red curry paste, and cook for 1-2 minutes, or until fragrant.

4. Add the coconut milk, vegetable broth, soy sauce, lime juice, and honey to the pot. Stir well to combine all the ingredients.

5. Bring the soup to a simmer, then reduce the heat to low and cook for 15-20 minutes, or until the vegetables are cooked through and the flavors have melded together.

6. Season the Thai coconut vegetable soup with salt and pepper to taste.

7. Ladle the soup into bowls, and garnish with chopped fresh cilantro and lime wedges if desired.

8. Serve the Thai coconut vegetable soup hot as a delicious and comforting meal.

Enjoy this aromatic and flavorful Thai coconut vegetable soup as a nourishing and satisfying dish. Adjust the seasoning according to your taste preferences, and feel free to customize the recipe with additional ingredients like tofu, mushrooms, or bok choy.

## Sesame-Ginger Tat Soi

**Cooking Time:** Approximately 15 minutes

**Nutritional Information (per serving - serves 4):**

- Calories: 110 kcal

- Protein: 3g

- Carbohydrates: 8g

- Fat: 8g

- Fiber: 2g

- Sodium: 200mg

**Ingredients:**

- 1 tablespoon sesame oil

- 2 cloves garlic, minced

- 1 tablespoon fresh ginger, grated

- 1 bunch tat soi, trimmed and chopped

- 2 tablespoons soy sauce (gluten-free if needed)

- 1 tablespoon rice vinegar

- 1 teaspoon honey

- 1 tablespoon sesame seeds, toasted

- Optional garnish: sliced green onions

## Instructions:

1. Heat the sesame oil over medium heat, in a large skillet. Add the minced garlic and grated ginger, and sauté for 1-2 minutes, or until fragrant.

2. Add the chopped tat soi to the skillet. Stir well to coat the greens with the sesame oil, garlic, and ginger.

3. In a small bowl, whisk together the soy sauce, rice vinegar, and honey. Pour the mixture over the tat soi in the skillet.

4. Cook the tat soi for 3-5 minutes, or until the greens are wilted but still bright green.

5. Once cooked, remove the tat soi from the heat and transfer it to a serving platter.

6. Sprinkle the toasted sesame seeds over the tat soi.

7. Garnish the sesame-ginger tat soi with sliced green onions if desired.

8. Serve the sesame-ginger tat soi hot as a delicious and nutritious side dish.

Enjoy this flavorful and vibrant sesame-ginger tat soi as a delicious and nutritious addition to your meals. Adjust the seasoning according to your taste preferences, and feel free to customize the recipe with additional ingredients like sliced mushrooms, bell peppers, or snow peas.

## Romanesco Tabouli

**Cooking Time:** Approximately 30 minutes

**Nutritional Information (per serving - serves 4):**

- Calories: 180 kcal

- Protein: 5g

- Carbohydrates: 20g

- Fat: 10g

- Fiber: 5g

- Sodium: 250mg

**Ingredients:**

- 1 small head romanesco, florets separated

- 1 cup quinoa, rinsed and drained

- 2 cups vegetable broth

- 1/4 cup extra-virgin olive oil

- 2 tablespoons fresh lemon juice

- 1 clove garlic, minced

- 1/4 cup fresh parsley, chopped

- 1/4 cup fresh mint leaves, chopped

- 1/4 cup cherry tomatoes, halved

- Salt and pepper to taste

**Instructions:**

1. In a medium pot, combine the rinsed and drained quinoa and vegetable broth. Bring the mixture to a boil, then reduce the heat to low, cover the pot, and simmer for 15-20 minutes, or until the quinoa is cooked through and the liquid is absorbed.

2. While the quinoa is cooking, bring a pot of water to a boil. Add the romanesco florets to the boiling water and blanch for 2-3 minutes, or until they are tender-crisp. Drain the romanesco and rinse it under cold water to stop the cooking process.

3. Once cooked, transfer the quinoa to a large bowl and let it cool slightly.

4. In a small bowl, whisk together the extra-virgin olive oil, fresh lemon juice, minced garlic,

chopped parsley, and chopped mint leaves.

5. Add the blanched romanesco florets and halved cherry tomatoes to the bowl with the quinoa.

6. Pour the dressing over the quinoa, romanesco, and cherry tomatoes, and toss until everything is evenly coated.

7. Season the Romanesco tabouli with salt and pepper to taste.

8. Serve the Romanesco tabouli warm or at room temperature.

Enjoy this vibrant and flavorful Romanesco tabouli as a delicious and nutritious side dish or light meal. Adjust the seasoning according to your taste preferences, and feel free to customize the recipe with additional ingredients like diced cucumber, red onion, or olives.

## Japanese Cucumber Salad

**Cooking Time:** Approximately 10 minutes

**Nutritional Information (per serving - serves 4):**

- Calories: 40 kcal

- Protein: 1g

- Carbohydrates: 5g

- Fat: 2g

- Fiber: 1g

- Sodium: 150mg

## Ingredients:

- 2 Japanese cucumbers, thinly sliced

- 1 tablespoon rice vinegar

- 1 teaspoon soy sauce (gluten-free if needed)

- 1/2 teaspoon sesame oil

- 1/2 teaspoon honey

- 1/4 teaspoon grated fresh ginger

- 1/4 teaspoon toasted sesame seeds

- Optional garnish: sliced green onions

## Instructions:

1. In a large bowl, combine the thinly sliced Japanese cucumbers.

2. In a small bowl, whisk together the rice vinegar, soy sauce, sesame oil, honey, and grated fresh ginger.

3. Pour the dressing over the Japanese cucumbers, and toss

until the cucumbers are evenly coated.

4. Sprinkle the toasted sesame seeds over the Japanese cucumber salad.

5. If desired, garnish the salad with sliced green onions.

6. Serve the Japanese cucumber salad immediately as a refreshing and light side dish.

Enjoy this crisp and flavorful Japanese cucumber salad as a delicious and nutritious addition to your meals. Adjust the seasoning according to your taste preferences, and feel free to customize the recipe with additional ingredients like sliced radishes, red onion, or bell peppers.

## Mediterranean Vegetable Stew

**Cooking Time:** Approximately 35 minutes

**Nutritional Information (per serving - serves 4):**

- Calories: 160 kcal

- Protein: 4g

- Carbohydrates: 18g

- Fat: 9g

- Fiber: 5g

- Sodium: 460mg

## Ingredients:

- 2 tablespoons olive oil

- 1 small onion, finely chopped

- 2 cloves garlic, minced

- 1 small eggplant, diced

- 1 small zucchini, diced

- 1 small yellow squash, diced

- 1 red bell pepper, diced

- 1 can of diced tomatoes with juices (14 ounces)

- 1 can of drained and rinsed chickpeas (14 ounces)

- 1/2 cup vegetable broth

- 1 teaspoon dried oregano

- 1 teaspoon dried basil

- 1/2 teaspoon dried thyme

- 1/2 teaspoon smoked paprika

- Salt and pepper to taste

- Chopped fresh parsley for garnish

**Instructions:**

1. Heat the olive oil over medium heat, in a large pot Add the already chopped onion and the minced garlic, and you sauté for about 2-3 minutes, or until the onion is soft and translucent.

2. Add the diced eggplant, zucchini, yellow squash, and red bell pepper to the pot. Sauté for an additional 3-4 minutes, or until the vegetables are slightly tender.

3. Stir in the diced tomatoes (with juices), drained and rinsed chickpeas, vegetable broth, dried oregano, dried basil, dried thyme, and smoked paprika.

4. Bring the mixture to a simmer, then reduce the heat to low and cook for 20-25 minutes, or until the vegetables are cooked through and the flavors have melded together.

5. Season the Mediterranean vegetable stew with salt and pepper to taste.

6. Once cooked, remove the Mediterranean vegetable stew from the heat and let it cool for a few minutes before serving.

7. Serve the Mediterranean vegetable stew hot, garnished with chopped fresh parsley.

Enjoy this hearty and flavorful Mediterranean vegetable stew as a delicious and nutritious main course. Adjust the seasoning according to your taste preferences, and feel free to customize the recipe with additional ingredients like diced carrots, celery, or potatoes.

## Spring Green Detox Soup

**Cooking Time:** Approximately 30 minutes

**Nutritional Information (per serving - serves 4):**

- Calories: 90 kcal

- Protein: 3g

- Carbohydrates: 10g

- Fat: 4g

- Fiber: 3g

- Sodium: 220mg

**Ingredients:**

- 1 tablespoon olive oil

- 1 small onion, finely chopped

- 2 cloves garlic, minced

- 1 small head broccoli, chopped

- 1 small zucchini, chopped

- 1 cup frozen green peas

- 1 cup spinach leaves

- 4 cups vegetable broth

- 1/4 teaspoon ground turmeric

- Salt and pepper to taste

- Optional garnish: chopped fresh parsley, lemon wedges

## Instructions:

1. Heat the olive oil over medium heat, in a large pot. Add the already chopped onion and the minced garlic, and you need to sauté for about 2-3 minutes, or until the onion is soft and translucent.

2. Add the chopped broccoli, chopped zucchini, and frozen green peas to the pot. Sauté for an additional 3-4 minutes, or until the vegetables are slightly tender.

3. Stir in the spinach leaves, vegetable broth, and ground turmeric.

4. Bring the mixture to a simmer, then reduce the heat to low and cook for 15-20 minutes, or until the vegetables are cooked through and the

flavors have melded together.

5. Season the spring green detox soup with salt and pepper to taste.

6. Once cooked, remove the soup from the heat and let it cool for a few minutes before serving.

7. Serve the spring green detox soup hot, garnished with chopped fresh parsley and lemon wedges if desired.

Enjoy this vibrant and nutritious spring green detox soup as a delicious and cleansing meal. Adjust the seasoning according to your taste preferences, and feel free to customize the recipe with additional ingredients like kale, Swiss chard, or celery.

## Strawberry-Chai Fruit Salad

**Cooking Time:** Approximately 10 minutes

**Nutritional Information (per serving - serves 4):**

- Calories: 90 kcal

- Protein: 1g

- Carbohydrates: 20g

- Fat: 1g

- Fiber: 3g

- Sodium: 0mg

## Ingredients:

- 1 cup strawberries, hulled and quartered

- 1 cup blueberries

- 1 cup raspberries

- 1 cup blackberries

- 1/2 teaspoon ground cinnamon

- 1/4 teaspoon ground cardamom

- 1/4 teaspoon ground cloves

- 1/4 teaspoon ground ginger

- 1/4 teaspoon ground allspice

- 1/4 teaspoon ground nutmeg

- 1 tablespoon honey

- 1 tablespoon fresh lemon juice

- 1 tablespoon fresh orange juice

- Optional garnish: chopped fresh mint leaves

## Instructions:

1. In a large bowl, combine the hulled and quartered strawberries, blueberries, raspberries, and blackberries.

2. In a small bowl, whisk together the ground cinnamon, ground cardamom, ground cloves, ground ginger, ground allspice, and ground nutmeg.

3. Sprinkle the spice mixture over the mixed berries, and toss until the berries are evenly coated.

4. In a separate small bowl, whisk together the honey, fresh lemon juice, and fresh orange juice.

5. Pour the honey-lemon-orange juice mixture over the mixed berries, and toss until the berries are evenly coated.

6. Cover the bowl with plastic wrap and refrigerate for at least 30 minutes to allow the flavors to meld together.

7. Once chilled, remove the strawberry-chai fruit salad from the refrigerator and give it a final stir.

8. If desired, garnish the salad with chopped fresh mint leaves before serving.

9. Serve the strawberry-chai fruit salad cold as a refreshing and nutritious dessert or snack.

Enjoy this vibrant and flavorful strawberry-chai fruit salad as a delicious and healthy addition to your meals. Adjust the seasoning according to your taste preferences, and feel free to customize the recipe with additional ingredients like sliced kiwi, pineapple, or mango.

# CHAPTER FOUR: BEVERAGES/SMOOTHIES RECIPES

Beverages and smoothies are a delightful and refreshing way to incorporate essential nutrients into your diet, especially if you are managing Eosinophilic Esophagitis (EOE). In this section of the EOE Diet Cookbook, we explore a variety of liquid recipes designed to provide nourishment while adhering to the Six Food Elimination Diet. Our collection features beverages and smoothies free from gluten, dairy, eggs, fish, soy, and nuts, aiming to cater to the dietary needs of EOE patients. From vibrant fruit smoothies to soothing herbal teas, these recipes offer a spectrum of flavors and health benefits. Let's embark on a journey of liquid nourishment and hydration with these beverage and smoothie recipes!

## Blueberry Cabbage Detox Smoothie

**Cooking Time:** Approximately 5 minutes

**Nutritional Information (per serving - serves 1):**

- Calories: 130 kcal

- Protein: 2g

- Carbohydrates: 25g

- Fat: 3g

- Fiber: 7g

- Sodium: 20mg

## Ingredients:

- 1/2 cup frozen blueberries

- 1/2 cup shredded purple cabbage

- 1/2 cup baby spinach leaves

- 1 small banana, peeled and frozen

- 1 tablespoon chia seeds

- 1/2 cup of unsweetened almond milk or any other milk of your choice

- 1/2 cup water

- Optional: 1 tablespoon honey or maple syrup for added sweetness

## Instructions:

1. In a blender, combine the frozen blueberries, shredded purple cabbage, baby spinach leaves, frozen banana, chia seeds, unsweetened almond milk, and water.

2. If desired, add honey or maple syrup for added sweetness.

3. Blend the ingredients on high speed until smooth and creamy.

4. Taste the blueberry cabbage detox smoothie and adjust the sweetness to your liking, adding more honey or maple syrup if desired.

5. Once blended to your desired consistency, pour the blueberry cabbage detox smoothie into a glass and serve immediately.

Enjoy this vibrant and nutritious blueberry cabbage detox smoothie as a delicious and refreshing beverage. Adjust the sweetness and consistency according to your taste preferences, and feel free to customize the recipe with additional ingredients like Greek yogurt, protein powder, or flaxseed.

## Citrus Green Smoothie

**Cooking Time:** Approximately 5 minutes

**Nutritional Information (per serving - serves 1):**

- Calories: 150 kcal

- Protein: 4g

- Carbohydrates: 30g

- Fat: 2g

- Fiber: 5g

- Sodium: 20mg

## Ingredients:

- 1 small orange, peeled and segmented

- 1 small kiwi, peeled and chopped

- 1/2 small banana, peeled and chopped

- 1 cup baby spinach leaves

- 1/2 cup unsweetened almond milk or any other milk of choice

- 1/2 cup water

- 1 tablespoon chia seeds

- Optional: 1 tablespoon honey or maple syrup for added sweetness

## Instructions:

1. In a blender, combine the peeled and segmented orange, chopped kiwi, chopped banana, baby spinach leaves, unsweetened almond

milk, water, and chia seeds.

2. If desired, add honey or maple syrup for added sweetness.

3. Blend the ingredients on high speed until smooth and creamy.

4. Taste the citrus green smoothie and adjust the sweetness to your liking, adding more honey or maple syrup if desired.

5. Once blended to your desired consistency, pour the citrus green smoothie into a glass and serve immediately.

Enjoy this refreshing and nutrient-packed citrus green smoothie as a delicious and energizing beverage. Adjust the sweetness and consistency according to your taste preferences, and feel free to customize the recipe with additional ingredients like Greek yogurt, protein powder, or flaxseed.

## Refreshing Raspberry Ginger Smoothie

**Cooking Time:** Approximately 5 minutes

**Nutritional Information (per serving - serves 1):**

- Calories: 150 kcal

- Protein: 3g

- Carbohydrates: 30g

- Fat: 2g

- Fiber: 6g

- Sodium: 20mg

## Ingredients:

- 1/2 cup frozen raspberries

- 1/2 cup frozen pineapple chunks

- 1 small banana, peeled and frozen

- 1 tablespoon of fresh ginger, it should be peeled and grated

- 1/2 cup of unsweetened almond milk or any other milk of choice

- 1/2 cup water

- 1 tablespoon chia seeds

- Optional: 1 tablespoon honey or maple syrup for added sweetness

## Instructions:

1. In a blender, combine the frozen raspberries, frozen pineapple chunks, frozen banana, grated fresh ginger, unsweetened almond

milk, water, and chia seeds.

2. If desired, add honey or maple syrup for added sweetness.

3. Blend the ingredients on high speed until smooth and creamy.

4. Taste the refreshing raspberry ginger smoothie and adjust the sweetness to your liking, adding more honey or maple syrup if desired.

5. Once blended to your desired consistency, pour the refreshing raspberry ginger smoothie into a glass and serve immediately.

Enjoy this invigorating and tangy raspberry ginger smoothie as a delightful and revitalizing beverage. Adjust the sweetness and consistency according to your taste preferences, and feel free to customize the recipe with additional ingredients like Greek yogurt, protein powder, or flaxseed.

## Citrus-Ginger Immunity Shots

**Cooking Time:** Approximately 5 minutes

**Nutritional Information (per serving - serves 1):**

- Calories: 25 kcal

- Protein: 1g

- Carbohydrates: 6g

- Fat: 0g

- Fiber: 1g

- Sodium: 0mg

## Ingredients:

- 1 small orange, peeled and segmented

- 1 small lemon, peeled and segmented

- 1 small lime, peeled and segmented

- 1 tablespoon of very fresh ginger, it should be peeled and well grated

- Optional: 1 tablespoon honey or maple syrup for added sweetness

## Instructions:

1. In a blender or food processor, combine the peeled and segmented orange, lemon, and lime.

2. Add the grated fresh ginger to the blender or food processor.

3. If desired, add honey or maple syrup for added sweetness.

4. Blend the ingredients on high

speed until smooth and well combined.

5. Once blended, pour the citrus-ginger immunity shot into a small glass.

6. Serve the citrus-ginger immunity shot immediately.

Enjoy this zesty and invigorating citrus-ginger immunity shot as a potent and refreshing beverage. Adjust the sweetness according to your taste preferences, and feel free to customize the recipe with additional ingredients like turmeric, cayenne pepper, or cinnamon.

## Cranberry Ginger Mocktail

**Cooking Time:** Approximately 5 minutes

**Nutritional Information (per serving - serves 1):**

- Calories: 50 kcal

- Protein: 0g

- Carbohydrates: 13g

- Fat: 0g

- Fiber: 1g

- Sodium: 0mg

## Ingredients:

- 1/2 cup unsweetened cranberry juice

- 1 tablespoon fresh ginger, peeled and grated

- 1 tablespoon fresh lemon juice

- 1/2 cup sparkling water

- Ice cubes

- Optional: 1 tablespoon honey or maple syrup for added sweetness

- Optional garnish: lemon or lime wedge, fresh cranberries, mint leaves

## Instructions:

1. In a small saucepan, combine the unsweetened cranberry juice and grated fresh ginger.

2. If desired, add honey or maple syrup for added sweetness.

3. Bring the mixture to a simmer over medium heat, then reduce the heat to low and let it simmer for 2-3 minutes, or until the flavors have melded together.

4. Once simmered, remove the cranberry-ginger mixture from the heat and let it cool for a few minutes.

5. In a glass, combine the fresh lemon juice and sparkling water.

6. Add the cooled cranberry-ginger mixture to the glass, and stir well to combine.

7. Add ice cubes to the glass, and garnish with a lemon or lime wedge, fresh cranberries, or mint leaves if desired.

8. Serve the cranberry ginger mocktail immediately.

Enjoy this refreshing and tangy cranberry ginger mocktail as a delightful and festive beverage. Adjust the sweetness according to your taste preferences, and feel free to customize the recipe with additional ingredients like orange juice, pomegranate juice, or cinnamon.

## Pineapple-Cucumber-Mint Smoothie

**Cooking Time:** Approximately 5 minutes

**Nutritional Information (per serving - serves 1):**

- Calories: 110 kcal

- Protein: 2g

- Carbohydrates: 25g

- Fat: 1g

- Fiber: 5g

- Sodium: 0mg

## Ingredients:

- 1/2 cup frozen pineapple chunks

- 1/2 cup cucumber, peeled and chopped

- 1/2 cup fresh mint leaves

- 1/2 cup unsweetened almond milk (or any milk of choice)

- 1/2 cup water

- 1 tablespoon chia seeds

- Optional: 1 tablespoon honey or maple syrup for added sweetness

## Instructions:

1. In a blender, combine the frozen pineapple chunks, chopped cucumber, fresh mint leaves, unsweetened almond milk, water, and chia seeds.

2. If desired, add honey or maple syrup for added sweetness.

3. Blend the ingredients on high

speed until smooth and creamy.

4. Taste the pineapple-cucumber-mint smoothie and adjust the sweetness to your liking, adding more honey or maple syrup if desired.

5. Once blended to your desired consistency, pour the pineapple-cucumber-mint smoothie into a glass and serve immediately.

Enjoy this refreshing and hydrating pineapple-cucumber-mint smoothie as a delicious and revitalizing beverage. Adjust the sweetness and consistency according to your taste preferences, and feel free to customize the recipe with additional ingredients like spinach, kale, or Greek yogurt.

## Honeydew-Cucumber Slushies

**Cooking Time:** Approximately 5 minutes

**Nutritional Information (per serving - serves 1):**

- Calories: 60 kcal

- Protein: 1g

- Carbohydrates: 15g

- Fat: 0g

- Fiber: 1g

- Sodium: 0mg

## Ingredients:

- 1 cup honeydew melon, peeled, seeded, and chopped

- 1/2 cup cucumber, peeled and chopped

- 1/2 cup water

- 1 tablespoon fresh lime juice

- 1 tablespoon honey or maple syrup

- Optional: 1/2 cup ice cubes for a slushier texture

- Optional garnish: mint leaves, lime wedges

## Instructions:

1. In a blender, combine the chopped honeydew melon, chopped cucumber, water, fresh lime juice, and honey or maple syrup.

2. If desired, add ice cubes for a slushier texture.

3. Blend the ingredients on high speed until smooth and well combined.

4. Once blended, pour the honeydew-

cucumber slushies into glasses.

5. If desired, garnish the slushies with mint leaves and lime wedges.

6. Serve the honeydew-cucumber slushies immediately.

Enjoy these refreshing and hydrating honeydew-cucumber slushies as a delightful and revitalizing beverage. Adjust the sweetness and consistency according to your taste preferences, and feel free to customize the recipe with additional ingredients like mint leaves, basil leaves, or ginger.

## Celery-Ginger Juice

**Cooking Time:** Approximately 5 minutes

**Nutritional Information (per serving - serves 1):**

- Calories: 30 kcal

- Protein: 1g

- Carbohydrates: 7g

- Fat: 0g

- Fiber: 2g

- Sodium: 100mg

**Ingredients:**

- 4 large celery stalks, chopped

- 1 tablespoon of fresh ginger, it should be peeled and grated

- 1 small apple, cored and chopped

- 1 small lemon, peeled and segmented

- 1/2 cup water

- Optional: 1 tablespoon honey or maple syrup for added sweetness

**Instructions:**

1. In a blender or food processor, combine the chopped celery stalks, grated fresh ginger, chopped apple, segmented lemon, and water.

2. If desired, add honey or maple syrup for added sweetness.

3. Blend the ingredients on high speed until smooth and well combined.

4. Once blended, pour the celery-ginger juice through a fine-mesh strainer or cheesecloth into a glass to remove any pulp.

5. Serve the celery-ginger juice immediately.

Enjoy this refreshing and invigorating

celery-ginger juice as a delightful and hydrating beverage. Adjust the sweetness according to your taste preferences, and feel free to customize the recipe with additional ingredients like cucumber, spinach, or lime juice.

## Icy Matcha-Banana Smoothie

**Cooking Time:** Approximately 5 minutes

**Nutritional Information (per serving - serves 1):**

- Calories: 120 kcal

- Protein: 2g

- Carbohydrates: 25g

- Fat: 2g

- Fiber: 3g

- Sodium: 0mg

**Ingredients:**

- 1/2 cup of unsweetened almond milk or any other milk of choice

- 1/2 cup water

- 1 tablespoon matcha powder

- 1 small banana, peeled and frozen

- 1/2 cup ice cubes

- Optional: 1 tablespoon honey or maple syrup for added sweetness

## Instructions:

1. In a blender, combine the unsweetened almond milk, water, matcha powder, frozen banana, and ice cubes.

2. If desired, add honey or maple syrup for added sweetness.

3. Blend the ingredients on high speed until smooth and creamy.

4. Taste the icy matcha-banana smoothie and adjust the sweetness to your liking, adding more honey or maple syrup if desired.

5. Once blended to your desired consistency, pour the icy matcha-banana smoothie into a glass and serve immediately.

Enjoy this refreshing and energizing icy matcha-banana smoothie as a delightful and revitalizing beverage. Adjust the sweetness and consistency according to your taste preferences, and feel free to customize the recipe with additional ingredients like spinach, kale, or Greek yogurt.

## Blueberry Kale Protein Smoothie

**Cooking Time:** Approximately 5 minutes

**Nutritional Information (per serving - serves 1):**

- Calories: 200 kcal

- Protein: 10g

- Carbohydrates: 25g

- Fat: 7g

- Fiber: 6g

- Sodium: 130mg

**Ingredients:**

- 1/2 cup frozen blueberries

- 1 small banana, peeled and frozen

- 1/2 cup chopped kale leaves, stems removed

- 1/2 cup of unsweetened almond milk or any other milk of your choice

- 1/2 cup water

- 1 scoop protein powder (vanilla or unflavored)

- 1 tablespoon chia seeds

- Optional: 1 tablespoon honey or maple syrup for added sweetness

## Instructions:

1. In a blender, combine the frozen blueberries, frozen banana, chopped kale leaves, unsweetened almond milk, water, protein powder, and chia seeds.

2. If desired, add honey or maple syrup for added sweetness.

3. Blend the ingredients on high speed until smooth and creamy.

4. Taste the blueberry kale protein smoothie and adjust the sweetness to your liking, adding more honey or maple syrup if desired.

5. Once blended to your desired consistency, pour the blueberry kale protein smoothie into a glass and serve immediately.

Enjoy this nutritious and satisfying blueberry kale protein smoothie as a delicious and energizing beverage. Adjust the sweetness and consistency according to your taste preferences, and feel free to customize the recipe with additional ingredients like spinach, Greek yogurt, or flaxseed.

## Watermelon Lemonade

**Cooking Time:** Approximately 10 minutes

**Nutritional Information (per serving - serves 4):**

- Calories: 80 kcal

- Protein: 1g

- Carbohydrates: 20g

- Fat: 0g

- Fiber: 1g

- Sodium: 0mg

**Ingredients:**

- 4 cups cubed seedless watermelon

- 1/2 cup fresh lemon juice

- 1/4 cup honey or maple syrup

- 4 cups cold water

- Ice cubes

- Fresh mint leaves for garnish

- Lemon slices for garnish

## Instructions:

1. In a blender, combine the cubed seedless watermelon, fresh lemon juice, and honey or maple syrup.

2. Blend the ingredients on high speed until smooth and well combined.

3. Once blended, pour the watermelon lemonade through a fine-mesh strainer or cheesecloth into a large pitcher to remove any pulp.

4. Add the cold water to the pitcher and stir well to combine.

5. Fill glasses with ice cubes, and pour the watermelon lemonade into the glasses.

6. If desired, garnish each glass with fresh mint leaves and lemon slices.

7. Serve the watermelon lemonade immediately.

Enjoy this refreshing and hydrating watermelon lemonade as a delightful and revitalizing beverage. Adjust the sweetness according to your taste preferences, and feel free to customize the recipe with additional ingredients like fresh lime juice, basil leaves, or ginger.

# Pineapple Mint Smoothie

**Cooking Time:** Approximately 5 minutes

**Nutritional Information (per serving - serves 1):**

- Calories: 150 kcal

- Protein: 2g

- Carbohydrates: 35g

- Fat: 1g

- Fiber: 4g

- Sodium: 0mg

**Ingredients:**

- 1/2 cup frozen pineapple chunks

- 1/2 cup cucumber, peeled and chopped

- 1/2 cup fresh mint leaves

- 1/2 cup of unsweetened almond milk or any other milk of your choice

- 1/2 cup water

- 1 tablespoon chia seeds

- Optional: 1 tablespoon honey or maple syrup for added sweetness

**Instructions:**

1. In a blender, combine the frozen

pineapple chunks, chopped cucumber, fresh mint leaves, unsweetened almond milk, water, and chia seeds.

2. If desired, add honey or maple syrup for added sweetness.

3. Blend the ingredients on high speed until smooth and creamy.

4. Taste the pineapple mint smoothie and adjust the sweetness to your liking, adding more honey or maple syrup if desired.

5. Once blended to your desired consistency, pour the pineapple mint smoothie into a glass and serve immediately.

Enjoy this refreshing and hydrating pineapple mint smoothie as a delightful and revitalizing beverage. Adjust the sweetness and consistency according to your taste preferences, and feel free to customize the recipe with additional ingredients like spinach, kale, or Greek yogurt.

# CHAPTER FIVE: KITCHEN STAPLES

Kitchen staples are essential ingredients that form the foundation of any Eosinophilic Esophagitis (EOE) diet. In this section of the EOE Diet Cookbook, we explore a variety of pantry and refrigerator staples designed to provide nourishment while adhering to the Six Food Elimination Diet. From gluten-free flours and dairy-free milk alternatives to nut-free oils and soy-free condiments, these staples offer a diverse array of flavors and culinary possibilities. Let's embark on a journey of nourishment and culinary creativity with these kitchen staples!

## Low Oxalate Chicken Broth

**Cooking Time:** This is approximately 1 hour and 30 minutes

**Nutritional Information (per serving - serves 6):**

- Calories: 15 kcal

- Protein: 1g

- Carbohydrates: 2g

- Fat: 0g

- Fiber: 0g

- Sodium: 90mg

## Ingredients:

- 2 pounds chicken bones (backs, necks, or wings)

- 1 onion, peeled and quartered

- 2 carrots, peeled and chopped

- 2 celery stalks, chopped

- 4 garlic cloves, peeled and smashed

- 1 teaspoon whole black peppercorns

- 1 bay leaf

- 1 teaspoon salt

- 8 cups water

## Instructions:

1. In a large pot, combine the chicken bones, onion, carrots, celery, garlic cloves, whole black peppercorns, bay leaf, salt, and water.

2. Over high heat, bring the mixture to a boil.

3. Once boiling, reduce the heat to low and let the broth simmer gently for 1 hour and 30 minutes,

or until the chicken bones are fully cooked and the broth is flavorful.

4. Skim any foam or impurities that rise to the surface of the broth with a spoon.

5. Once simmered, remove the pot from the heat and let the broth cool slightly.

6. Strain the broth through a fine-mesh strainer or cheesecloth into a large bowl to remove any solids.

7. Once strained, transfer the low oxalate chicken broth to airtight containers or jars, and refrigerate for up to 4 days or freeze for up to 3 months.

8. Use the low oxalate chicken broth as a base for soups, stews, sauces, or any other recipes that call for broth.

Enjoy this flavorful and versatile low oxalate chicken broth as a delicious and nourishing addition to your Eosinophilic Esophagitis (EOE) diet. Adjust the seasoning according to your taste preferences, and feel free to customize the recipe with additional ingredients like leeks, parsley, or thyme.

# Homemade Pumpkin Seed Butter

**Cooking Time:** Approximately 15 minutes

**Nutritional Information (per serving - serves 16):**

- Calories: 95 kcal

- Protein: 4g

- Carbohydrates: 2g

- Fat: 8g

- Fiber: 1g

- Sodium: 5mg

## Ingredients:

- 2 cups raw pumpkin seeds (pepitas)

- 1 tablespoon neutral-tasting oil (such as sunflower or grapeseed oil)

- 1/2 teaspoon salt (optional)

- Optional: 1 tablespoon honey or maple syrup for added sweetness

## Instructions:

1. Preheat the oven to 350°F (175°C).

2. Spread the raw pumpkin seeds (pepitas) in a single layer on a baking sheet lined with parchment paper.

3. Toast the pumpkin seeds in the preheated oven for 10-12 minutes, or until lightly golden brown and fragrant.

4. Once toasted, remove the pumpkin seeds from the oven and let them cool for a few minutes.

5. In a food processor or high-speed blender, combine the toasted pumpkin seeds, neutral-tasting oil, and salt (if using).

6. Blend the ingredients on high speed until smooth and creamy, scraping down the sides of the food processor or blender as needed.

7. If desired, add honey or maple syrup for added sweetness, and blend again until well combined.

8. Once blended to your desired consistency, transfer the homemade pumpkin seed butter to an airtight container or jar.

9. Store the homemade pumpkin seed butter in the refrigerator for up to 2 weeks.

10. Use the homemade pumpkin seed butter as a spread on toast, crackers, or fruit, or as an ingredient in

sauces, dips, or baked goods.

Enjoy this creamy and nutty homemade pumpkin seed butter as a delicious and nutritious addition to your Eosinophilic Esophagitis (EOE) diet. Adjust the sweetness and consistency according to your taste preferences, and feel free to customize the recipe with additional ingredients like cinnamon, nutmeg, or vanilla extract.

## Homemade Grain-Free Baking Powder

**Cooking Time:** Approximately 5 minutes

**Nutritional Information (per serving - serves 32):**

- Calories: 0 kcal

- Protein: 0g

- Carbohydrates: 0g

- Fat: 0g

- Fiber: 0g

- Sodium: 100mg

## Ingredients:

- 1/4 cup cream of tartar

- 2 tablespoons baking soda

- 2 tablespoons of arrowroot starch or even tapioca starch

- 1 teaspoon salt

## Instructions:

1. In a small bowl, combine the cream of tartar, baking soda, arrowroot starch or tapioca starch, and salt.

2. Stir the ingredients together until well combined.

3. Transfer the homemade grain-free baking powder to an airtight container or jar.

4. Store the homemade grain-free baking powder in a cool, dry place for up to 6 months.

5. Use the homemade grain-free baking powder as a leavening agent in your grain-free baked goods, such as muffins, pancakes, waffles, or bread.

Enjoy this homemade grain-free baking powder as a convenient and versatile ingredient in your Eosinophilic Esophagitis (EOE) diet. Adjust the amount of baking powder according to your recipe's requirements, and feel free to customize the recipe with additional ingredients like cinnamon, nutmeg, or vanilla extract.

## Garlic Infused Olive Oil

**Cooking Time:** Approximately 5 minutes

**Nutritional Information (per serving - serves 16):**

- Calories: 120 kcal

- Protein: 0g

- Carbohydrates: 0g

- Fat: 14g

- Fiber: 0g

- Sodium: 0mg

**Ingredients:**

- 2 cups extra virgin olive oil

- 6 garlic cloves, peeled and smashed

- Optional: 1 teaspoon red pepper flakes for added spice

**Instructions:**

1. In a small saucepan, combine the extra virgin olive oil, smashed garlic cloves, and red pepper flakes (if using).

2. Heat the mixture over low heat until the garlic cloves begin to sizzle.

3. Once sizzling, reduce the heat to very low and let the garlic infuse the olive oil for 5 minutes, or until the garlic is lightly golden brown and fragrant.

4. Once infused, remove the saucepan from the heat and let the garlic infused olive oil cool for a few minutes.

5. Strain the garlic infused olive oil through a fine-mesh strainer or cheesecloth into a glass jar to remove the garlic cloves and red pepper flakes.

6. Once strained, transfer the garlic infused olive oil to an airtight container or jar.

7. Store the garlic infused olive oil in the refrigerator for up to 2 weeks.

8. Use the garlic infused olive oil as a flavorful and aromatic ingredient in your Eosinophilic Esophagitis (EOE)

diet, such as in salad dressings, marinades, sauces, or as a finishing oil for roasted vegetables or grilled meats.

Enjoy this rich and aromatic garlic infused olive oil as a versatile and delicious addition to your Eosinophilic Esophagitis (EOE) diet. Adjust the amount of garlic cloves and red pepper flakes according to your taste preferences, and feel free to customize the recipe with additional ingredients like fresh herbs, lemon zest, or black pepper.

## Sun Dried Tomatoes

**Cooking Time:** Approximately 3 hours

**Nutritional Information (per serving - serves 16):**

- Calories: 45 kcal

- Protein: 2g

- Carbohydrates: 11g

- Fat: 0g

- Fiber: 2g

- Sodium: 30mg


Recipe: Sun-Dried Tomatoes


Ingredients:

- 2 pounds ripe tomatoes (such as Roma or San Marzano), halved lengthwise and seeded

- 1 teaspoon salt

- Optional: 2 tablespoons olive oil, for drizzling

- Optional: 1 tablespoon fresh herbs (such as thyme, rosemary, or oregano), chopped


**Instructions:**

1. Preheat the oven to 200°F (95°C).

2. Line a baking sheet up using a parchment paper.

3. Place the halved and seeded tomatoes on the prepared baking sheet, cut side up.

4. Sprinkle the tomatoes with salt.

5. If desired, drizzle the tomatoes with olive oil and sprinkle with fresh herbs.

6. Place the baking sheet in the already preheated oven and what you need to do next is to bake the tomatoes for about 3 hours, or until they are dried and slightly shriveled.

7. Once dried, remove the baking sheet from the oven and let the sun-dried tomatoes cool completely.

8. Once cooled, transfer the sun-dried tomatoes to an airtight container or jar.

9. Store the sun-dried tomatoes in the refrigerator for up to 2 weeks, or freeze for up to 6 months.

10. Use the sun-dried tomatoes as a flavorful and versatile ingredient in your Eosinophilic Esophagitis (EOE) diet, such as in sauces, pasta dishes, salads, or as a topping for pizza or bruschetta.

Enjoy these rich and flavorful sun-dried tomatoes as a delicious and nutritious addition to your Eosinophilic Esophagitis (EOE) diet. Adjust the amount of salt and olive oil according to your taste preferences, and feel free to customize the recipe with additional ingredients like garlic, red pepper flakes, or balsamic vinegar.

# Black Current Vinegar

**Cooking Time:** Approximately 1 hour

**Nutritional Information (per serving - serves 32):**

- Calories: 10 kcal

- Protein: 0g

- Carbohydrates: 2g

- Fat: 0g

- Fiber: 0g

- Sodium: 0mg

## Ingredients:

- 4 cups black currants, washed and stems removed

- 4 cups white wine vinegar or apple cider vinegar

- Optional: 1 cup sugar or honey for added sweetness

## Instructions:

1. In a large glass or ceramic bowl, combine the black

currants and white wine vinegar or apple cider vinegar.

2. If desired, add sugar or honey for added sweetness.

3. Cover the bowl with a clean kitchen towel or cheesecloth and let the black currants and vinegar mixture sit at room temperature for 24 hours.

4. After 24 hours, strain the black currants and vinegar mixture through a fine-mesh strainer or cheesecloth into a large saucepan, pressing on the black currants to extract as much liquid as possible.

5. Once strained, discard the black currants and bring the vinegar to a boil over high heat.

6. Once boiling, reduce the heat to low and let the vinegar simmer gently for 30-45 minutes, or until it has reduced by half and is slightly thickened.

7. Once simmered, remove the saucepan from the heat and let the black currant vinegar cool completely.

8. Once cooled, transfer the black currant vinegar to an airtight container or jar.

9. Store the black currant vinegar in a cool, dark place for up to 6 months.

10. Use the black currant vinegar as a flavorful and versatile ingredient in your Eosinophilic Esophagitis (EOE) diet, such as in salad dressings, marinades, sauces, or as a finishing vinegar for roasted vegetables or grilled meats.

Enjoy this tangy and aromatic black currant vinegar as a delightful and nutritious addition to your Eosinophilic Esophagitis (EOE) diet. Adjust the amount of sugar or honey according to your taste preferences, and feel free to customize the recipe with additional ingredients like fresh herbs, garlic, or shallots.

## Homemade Herbal Sea Salt

**Cooking Time:** Approximately 5 minutes

**Nutritional Information (per serving - serves 16):**

- Calories: 0 kcal

- Protein: 0g

- Carbohydrates: 0g

- Fat: 0g

- Fiber: 0g

- Sodium: 1000mg

## Ingredients:

- 1/2 cup coarse sea salt

- 2 tablespoons dried herbs (such as rosemary, thyme, sage, or oregano), finely chopped

- Optional: 1 teaspoon lemon or orange zest for added citrus flavor

## Instructions:

1. In a small bowl, combine the coarse sea salt, finely chopped dried herbs, and lemon or orange zest (if using).

2. Stir the ingredients together until well combined.

3. Transfer the homemade herbal sea salt to an airtight container or jar.

4. Store the homemade herbal sea salt in a cool, dark place for up to 6 months.

5. Use the homemade herbal sea salt as a flavorful and aromatic ingredient in your Eosinophilic Esophagitis (EOE) diet, such as in marinades, rubs, or as a finishing salt for

roasted vegetables or grilled meats.

Enjoy this fragrant and flavorful homemade herbal sea salt as a delicious and versatile addition to your Eosinophilic Esophagitis (EOE) diet. Adjust the amount of dried herbs according to your taste preferences, and feel free to customize the recipe with additional ingredients like garlic powder, onion powder, or red pepper flakes.

## Apple-Plum Sauce

**Cooking Time:** Approximately 30 minutes

**Nutritional Information (per serving - serves 16):**

- Calories: 40 kcal

- Protein: 0g

- Carbohydrates: 10g

- Fat: 0g

- Fiber: 2g

- Sodium: 0mg

## Ingredients:

- 4 large apples, peeled, cored, and chopped

- 4 large plums, pitted and chopped

- 1/4 cup water

- 1 tablespoon honey or maple syrup

- 1 teaspoon ground cinnamon

- 1/2 teaspoon ground ginger

- 1/4 teaspoon ground nutmeg

- 1/4 teaspoon ground cloves

- Optional: 1 tablespoon lemon juice for added tanginess

## Instructions:

1. In a large saucepan, combine the chopped apples, chopped plums, water, honey or maple syrup, ground cinnamon, ground ginger, ground nutmeg, and ground cloves.

2. If desired, add lemon juice for added tanginess.

3. Bring the mixture to boil over a very high heat.

4. Once boiling, reduce the heat to low and let the apple-plum sauce simmer gently for 20-30 minutes, or until the apples and plums are soft and the sauce has thickened.

5. Once simmered, remove the saucepan from the heat and let the apple-plum sauce cool for a few minutes.

6. Once cooled, transfer the apple-plum sauce to an airtight container or jar.

7. Store the apple-plum sauce in the refrigerator for up to 2 weeks.

8. Usc the apple-plum sauce as a flavorful and versatile ingredient in your Eosinophilic Esophagitis (EOE) diet, such as in oatmeal, yogurt, pancakes, or as a topping for ice cream or desserts.

Enjoy this sweet and spiced apple-plum sauce as a delightful and nutritious addition to your Eosinophilic Esophagitis (EOE) diet. Adjust the sweetness and spice level according to your taste preferences, and feel free to customize the recipe with additional ingredients like vanilla extract, orange zest, or raisins.

## Homemade Kombucha
**Cooking Time:** Approximately 10 days

**Nutritional Information (per serving - serves 16):**

- Calories: 0 kcal

- Protein: 0g

- Carbohydrates: 0g

- Fat: 0g

- Fiber: 0g

- Sodium: 10mg

**Ingredients:**

- 1 SCOBY (It means Symbiotic Culture of Bacteria and Yeast)

- 1 cup brewed black tea (room temperature)

- 1/4 cup granulated sugar

- 4 cups filtered water

- Optional: 1 cup fruit juice (such as apple, grape, or cranberry) for flavoring

**Instructions:**

1. In a large glass or ceramic container, combine the brewed black tea, granulated sugar, and filtered water.

2. Stir the mixture until the sugar has dissolved.

3. Carefully place the SCOBY on top of the tea mixture.

4. Cover the container with a clean kitchen towel or cheesecloth and secure it with a rubber band.

5. Let the homemade kombucha ferment at room temperature (70-80°F or 21-27°C) for 7-10 days, or until it has reached the desired level of tartness and carbonation.

6. Once fermented, carefully remove the SCOBY from the kombucha and transfer it to a clean glass or ceramic container with a small amount of the fermented kombucha.

7. If desired, strain the fermented kombucha through a fine-mesh strainer or cheesecloth into a large glass pitcher or jar.

8. If using fruit juice for flavoring, add the fruit juice to the fermented kombucha and stir well to combine.

9. Transfer the flavored homemade kombucha to airtight bottles or jars.

10. Store the homemade kombucha in the refrigerator for up to 2 weeks.

11. Enjoy the homemade kombucha as a refreshing and probiotic-rich beverage.

Enjoy this tangy and effervescent homemade kombucha as a delightful and nutritious addition to your Eosinophilic Esophagitis (EOE) diet. Adjust the fermentation time according to your taste preferences, and feel free to customize the recipe with additional ingredients like fresh ginger, lemon slices, or herbs.

# CHAPTER SIX: CONDIMENTS

Condiments are essential components of any Eosinophilic Esophagitis (EOE) diet, adding flavor and variety to meals while ensuring they are safe and allergen-free. In this section of the EOE Diet Cookbook, we explore a variety of homemade condiments that cater to the Six Food Elimination Diet, including ketchup, mustard, mayonnaise, and salad dressings. These condiments are free from gluten, dairy, eggs, fish, soy, and nuts, making them suitable for individuals with Eosinophilic Esophagitis and other food allergies. Let's discover the delicious world of allergen-free condiments and enhance our culinary creations!

## Creamy Tahini-Dill Dressing

**Cooking Time:** Approximately 5 minutes

**Nutritional Information (per serving - serves 16):**

- Calories: 45 kcal

- Protein: 1g

- Carbohydrates: 2g

- Fat: 4g

- Fiber: 0g

- Sodium: 60mg

## Ingredients:

- 1/4 cup tahini

- 1/4 cup lemon juice

- 1/4 cup water

- 1 tablespoon of extra virgin olive oil

- 1 tablespoon honey or maple syrup

- 1 teaspoon Dijon mustard

- 1 garlic clove, minced

- 1 tablespoon fresh dill, chopped

- Salt and black pepper to taste

## Instructions:

1. In a small bowl, whisk together the tahini, lemon juice, water, extra virgin olive oil, honey or maple syrup, Dijon mustard, and minced garlic until smooth and creamy.

2. Add the chopped fresh dill to the tahini mixture and whisk again until well combined.

3. Season the creamy tahini-dill dressing with salt and black pepper to taste.

4. Transfer the creamy tahini-dill dressing to an airtight container or jar.

5. Store the creamy tahini-dill dressing in the refrigerator for up to 1 week.

6. Use the creamy tahini-dill dressing as a flavorful and versatile ingredient in your Eosinophilic Esophagitis (EOE) diet, such as in salads, wraps, sandwiches, or as a dipping sauce for vegetables.

Enjoy this creamy and herbaceous tahini-dill dressing as a delicious and nutritious addition to your Eosinophilic Esophagitis (EOE) diet. Adjust the sweetness and acidity according to your taste preferences, and feel free to customize the recipe with additional ingredients like fresh parsley, cilantro, or mint.

## Basil-Avocado Sauce

**Cooking Time:** Approximately 5 minutes

**Nutritional Information (per serving - serves 16):**

- Calories: 50 kcal

- Protein: 1g

- Carbohydrates: 2g

- Fat: 4g

- Fiber: 1g

- Sodium: 60mg

## Ingredients:

- 1 ripe avocado, peeled and pitted

- 1/4 cup fresh basil leaves

- 1/4 cup extra virgin olive oil

- 1/4 cup water

- 1 tablespoon lemon juice

- 1 garlic clove, minced

- Salt and black pepper to taste

## Instructions:

1. In a food processor or high-speed blender, combine the ripe avocado, fresh basil leaves, extra virgin olive oil, water, lemon juice, and minced garlic.

2. Blend the ingredients on high speed until smooth and creamy, scraping down the sides of the

**134** | E O E   D I E T-
T h e   S i x   F o o d
E l i m i n a t i o n   D i e t .

food processor or blender as needed.

3. Season the basil-avocado sauce with salt and black pepper to taste.

4. Transfer the basil-avocado sauce to an airtight container or jar.

5. Store the basil-avocado sauce in the refrigerator for up to 3 days.

6. Use the basil-avocado sauce as a flavorful and versatile ingredient in your Eosinophilic Esophagitis (EOE) diet, such as in pasta dishes, sandwiches, wraps, or as a dipping sauce for vegetables.

Enjoy this creamy and herbaceous basil-avocado sauce as a delicious and nutritious addition to your Eosinophilic Esophagitis (EOE) diet. Adjust the acidity and seasoning according to your taste preferences, and feel free to customize the recipe with additional ingredients like fresh parsley, cilantro, or lime juice.

## Strawberry Salsa

**Cooking Time:** Approximately 15 minutes

## Nutritional Information (per serving - serves 16):

- Calories: 20 kcal

- Protein: 0g

- Carbohydrates: 5g

- Fat: 0g

- Fiber: 1g

- Sodium: 5mg

## Ingredients:

- 2 cups fresh strawberries, diced

- 1/4 cup red onion, finely chopped

- 1 jalapeno pepper, seeded and minced

- 1/4 cup fresh cilantro, chopped

- 1 tablespoon fresh lime juice

- 1 teaspoon honey or maple syrup

- Salt to taste

## Instructions:

1. In a medium bowl, combine the diced fresh strawberries, finely chopped red onion, minced jalapeno pepper, and chopped fresh cilantro.

2. In a small bowl, whisk together the fresh lime juice and honey or maple syrup until well combined.

3. Pour the lime juice mixture over the strawberry mixture and gently toss until everything is evenly coated.

4. Season the strawberry salsa with salt to taste.

5. Transfer the strawberry salsa to an airtight container or jar.

6. Store the strawberry salsa in the refrigerator for up to 3 days.

7. Use the strawberry salsa as a flavorful and versatile ingredient in your Eosinophilic Esophagitis (EOE) diet, such as in tacos, wraps, salads, or as a topping for grilled fish or chicken.

Enjoy this vibrant and refreshing strawberry salsa as a delicious and nutritious addition to your Eosinophilic Esophagitis (EOE) diet. Adjust the sweetness and spiciness according to your taste preferences, and feel free to customize the recipe with additional ingredients like diced mango, pineapple, or avocado.

# Creamy Coconut Ranch Dressing

**Cooking Time:** Approximately 5 minutes

**Nutritional Information (per serving - serves 16):**

- Calories: 50 kcal

- Protein: 1g

- Carbohydrates: 2g

- Fat: 4g

- Fiber: 0g

- Sodium: 60mg

**Ingredients:**

- 1/2 cup coconut milk (canned, full-fat)

- 1/2 cup mayonnaise (dairy-free)

- 1/4 cup fresh parsley, chopped

- 1 tablespoon fresh chives, chopped

- 1 tablespoon fresh dill, chopped

- 1 garlic clove, minced

- 1 tablespoon lemon juice

- Salt and black pepper to taste

## Instructions:

1. In a small bowl, whisk together the coconut milk, dairy-free mayonnaise, chopped fresh parsley, chopped fresh chives, chopped fresh dill, minced garlic clove, and lemon juice until smooth and creamy.

2. Season the creamy coconut ranch dressing with salt and black pepper to taste.

3. Transfer the creamy coconut ranch dressing to an airtight container or jar

4. Store the creamy coconut ranch dressing in the refrigerator for up to 1 week.

5. Use the creamy coconut ranch dressing as a flavorful and versatile ingredient in your Eosinophilic Esophagitis (EOE) diet, such as in salads, wraps, sandwiches, or as a dipping sauce for vegetables.

Enjoy this dairy-free and coconut-infused creamy ranch dressing as a delicious and nutritious addition to your Eosinophilic Esophagitis (EOE) diet. Adjust the herb ratio according to your taste preferences, and feel free to customize the recipe with additional ingredients like fresh cilantro, green onions, or lime juice.

## Thai/Massaman Curry Paste

**Cooking Time:** Approximately 15 minutes

**Nutritional Information (per serving - serves 16):**

- Calories: 25 kcal

- Protein: 1g

- Carbohydrates: 5g

- Fat: 0g

- Fiber: 1g

- Sodium: 10mg

**Ingredients:**

- 4 dried Thai bird's eye chilies, soaked in hot water for 10 minutes

- 1/4 cup fresh lemongrass, chopped

- 1/4 cup fresh galangal or ginger, chopped

- 1/4 cup fresh garlic, minced

- 1/4 cup fresh shallots, chopped

- 2 tablespoons fresh cilantro roots or stems, chopped

- 1 tablespoon shrimp paste (or 1 tablespoon soy sauce for vegetarian)

- 1 tablespoon ground coriander

- 1 teaspoon ground cumin

- 1 teaspoon ground cinnamon

- 1 teaspoon ground cloves

- 1 teaspoon ground cardamom

- 1 teaspoon ground turmeric

- 1/2 teaspoon ground nutmeg

- 1/4 teaspoon ground white pepper

- 1/4 teaspoon ground black pepper

- 1/4 cup water

**Instructions:**

1. In a food processor or high-speed blender, combine the soaked Thai bird's eye chilies, fresh lemongrass, fresh galangal or ginger, fresh garlic, fresh shallots, fresh cilantro roots or stems, shrimp paste (or soy sauce for vegetarian), ground coriander, ground cumin, ground cinnamon, ground cloves, ground cardamom, ground

turmeric, ground nutmeg, ground white pepper, ground black pepper, and water.

2. Blend the ingredients on high speed until a smooth and thick paste forms, scraping down the sides of the food processor or blender as needed.

3. Transfer the Thai/Massaman curry paste to an airtight container or jar.

4. Store the Thai/Massaman curry paste in the refrigerator for up to 1 week, or freeze for up to 3 months.

5. Use the Thai/Massaman curry paste as a flavorful and versatile ingredient in your Eosinophilic Esophagitis (EOE) diet, such as in curries, soups, stews, stir-fries, or as a marinade for meats or tofu.

Enjoy this fragrant and aromatic Thai/Massaman curry paste as a delicious and versatile addition to your Eosinophilic Esophagitis (EOE) diet. Adjust the spiciness and seasoning according to your taste preferences, and feel free to customize the recipe with additional ingredients like fresh lime leaves, kaffir lime zest, or Thai basil.

# Creamy Coconut Ranch Dressing

**Cooking Time:** Approximately 10 minutes

**Nutritional Information (per serving - serves 16):**

- Calories: 90 kcal

- Protein: 1g

- Carbohydrates: 2g

- Fat: 9g

- Fiber: 0g

- Sodium: 60mg

## Ingredients:

- 1/2 cup coconut cream

- 1/2 cup mayonnaise

- 1/4 cup fresh cilantro, chopped

- 1/4 cup fresh chives, chopped

- 1/4 cup fresh dill, chopped

- 2 garlic cloves, minced

- 1 tablespoon lemon juice

- 1 teaspoon honey or maple syrup

- Salt and black pepper to taste

## Instructions:

1. In a medium bowl, whisk together the coconut cream, mayonnaise, chopped fresh cilantro, chopped fresh chives, chopped fresh dill, minced garlic cloves, lemon juice, and honey or maple syrup until smooth and creamy.

2. Season the creamy coconut ranch dressing with salt and black pepper to taste.

3. Transfer the creamy coconut ranch dressing to an airtight container or jar.

4. Store the creamy coconut ranch dressing in the refrigerator for up to 1 week.

5. Use the creamy coconut ranch dressing as a flavorful and versatile ingredient in your Eosinophilic Esophagitis (EOE) diet, such as in salads, wraps, sandwiches, or as a dipping sauce for vegetables.

Enjoy this dairy-free and coconut-infused creamy ranch dressing as a delicious and nutritious addition to your Eosinophilic Esophagitis (EOE) diet. Adjust the herb ratio according to your taste preferences, and feel free to customize the recipe with additional ingredients like fresh parsley, green onions, or lime juice.

## Cherry Balsamic Vinargrette

**Cooking Time:** Approximately 5 minutes

**Nutritional Information (per serving - serves 16):**

- Calories: 40 kcal

- Protein: 0g

- Carbohydrates: 6g

- Fat: 2g

- Fiber: 0g

- Sodium: 5mg

**Ingredients:**

- 1/2 cup of very fresh cherries, it should be pitted and halved

- 1/4 cup balsamic vinegar

- 1/4 cup extra virgin olive oil

- 1 tablespoon honey or maple syrup

- 1 teaspoon Dijon mustard

- 1 garlic clove, minced

- Salt and black pepper to taste

**Instructions:**

1. In a small bowl, mash the fresh cherries with a fork or potato masher until they form a coarse paste.

2. Add the balsamic vinegar, extra virgin olive oil, honey or maple syrup, Dijon mustard, minced garlic clove, salt, and black pepper to the mashed cherries.

3. Whisk all the ingredients together until they are well or properly combined.

4. Transfer the cherry balsamic vinaigrette to an airtight container or jar.

5. Store the cherry balsamic vinaigrette in the refrigerator for up to 1 week.

6. Use the cherry balsamic vinaigrette as a flavorful and versatile ingredient in your Eosinophilic Esophagitis (EOE) diet, such as in salads, wraps, sandwiches, or as a marinade for meats or tofu.

Enjoy this tangy and fruity cherry balsamic vinaigrette as a delicious and nutritious addition to your Eosinophilic Esophagitis (EOE) diet. Adjust the sweetness and acidity according to your taste preferences, and feel free to customize the recipe with additional ingredients like fresh herbs, orange zest, or shallots.

## Apple-Cardamon Cranberry Sauce

**Cooking Time:** Approximately 15 minutes

**Nutritional Information (per serving - serves 16):**

- Calories: 60 kcal

- Protein: 0g

- Carbohydrates: 15g

- Fat: 0g

- Fiber: 1g

- Sodium: 5mg

**Ingredients:**

- 2 cups fresh cranberries

- 1/4 cup apple juice or apple cider

- 1/4 cup honey or maple syrup

- 1/2 teaspoon ground cardamom

- 1/4 teaspoon ground cinnamon

- 1/4 teaspoon ground nutmeg

- 1/4 teaspoon ground cloves

- 1/4 teaspoon ground ginger

- 1/4 teaspoon salt

- 1 apple, peeled, cored, and diced

- 1 teaspoon lemon zest

**Instructions:**

1. In a medium saucepan, combine the fresh cranberries, apple juice or apple cider, honey or maple syrup, ground cardamom, ground cinnamon, ground nutmeg, ground cloves, ground ginger, and salt.

2. Bring the mixture to boil over a medium-high heat.

3. Once boiling, reduce the heat to low and let the cranberry sauce simmer gently for 10-15 minutes, or until the cranberries have burst and the sauce has thickened.

4. Once simmered, remove the saucepan from the heat and let the cranberry sauce cool for a few minutes.

5. Once cooled, stir in the diced apple and lemon zest until well combined.

6. Transfer the apple-cardamom cranberry sauce to an airtight container or jar.

7. Store the apple-cardamom cranberry sauce in the refrigerator for up to 1 week.

8. Use the apple-cardamom cranberry sauce as a flavorful and versatile ingredient in your Eosinophilic Esophagitis (EOE) diet, such as in turkey sandwiches, wraps, salads, or as a topping for desserts like yogurt or ice cream.

Enjoy this fragrant and spiced apple-cardamom cranberry sauce as a delicious and nutritious addition to your Eosinophilic Esophagitis (EOE) diet. Adjust the sweetness and spice level according to your taste preferences, and feel free to customize the recipe with additional ingredients like orange zest, vanilla extract, or chopped nuts.

## Fresh Peach Salsa

**Cooking Time:** Approximately 15 minutes

## Nutritional Information (per serving - serves 16):

- Calories: 25 kcal

- Protein: 1g

- Carbohydrates: 5g

- Fat: 0g

- Fiber: 1g

- Sodium: 5mg

## Ingredients:

- 2 cups fresh peaches, diced

- 1/4 cup red onion, finely chopped

- 1 jalapeno pepper, seeded and minced

- 1/4 cup fresh cilantro, chopped

- 1 tablespoon fresh lime juice

- 1 teaspoon honey or maple syrup

- Salt to taste

## Instructions:

1. In a medium bowl, combine the diced fresh peaches, finely chopped red onion, minced jalapeno pepper, and chopped fresh cilantro.

2. In a small bowl, whisk together the fresh lime juice and honey or maple syrup until well combined.

3. Pour the lime juice mixture over the peach mixture and gently toss until everything is evenly coated.

4. Season the fresh peach salsa with salt to taste.

5. Transfer the fresh peach salsa to an airtight container or jar.

6. Store the fresh peach salsa in the refrigerator for up to 3 days.

7. Use the fresh peach salsa as a flavorful and versatile ingredient in your Eosinophilic Esophagitis (EOE) diet, such as in tacos, wraps, salads, or as a topping for grilled fish or chicken.

Enjoy this sweet and tangy fresh peach salsa as a delicious and nutritious addition to your Eosinophilic Esophagitis (EOE) diet. Adjust the sweetness and spiciness according to your taste preferences, and feel free to customize the recipe with additional ingredients like diced mango, pineapple, or avocado.

# Homemade Enchilada Sauce

**Cooking Time:** Approximately 20 minutes

**Nutritional Information (per serving - serves 16):**

- Calories: 20 kcal

- Protein: 1g

- Carbohydrates: 4g

- Fat: 0g

- Fiber: 1g

- Sodium: 210mg

**Ingredients:**

- 2 tablespoons olive oil

- 2 tablespoons of an all-purpose flour (gluten-free flour)

- 1 tablespoon chili powder

- 1/2 teaspoon ground cumin

- 1/2 teaspoon garlic powder

- 1/4 teaspoon onion powder

- 1/4 teaspoon dried oregano

- 1/4 teaspoon paprika

- 1/4 teaspoon salt

- 1/4 teaspoon ground black pepper

- 1/4 teaspoon ground cinnamon

- 1/4 teaspoon ground cloves

- 1/4 teaspoon ground nutmeg

- 1 cup vegetable broth (or chicken broth)

- 1 cup tomato sauce

- 1 tablespoon honey or maple syrup

- 1 teaspoon apple cider vinegar

## Instructions:

1. Over medium heat, in a medium saucepan, heat the olive oil.

2. Add the all-purpose flour and whisk constantly until the mixture turns golden brown, about 1-2 minutes.

3. Add the chili powder, ground cumin, garlic powder, onion powder, dried oregano, paprika, salt, ground black pepper, ground cinnamon, ground cloves, and ground nutmeg to the saucepan.

4. Whisk the spices into the flour mixture until well combined.

5. Slowly pour in the vegetable broth (or chicken broth) while whisking continuously to prevent lumps from forming.

6. Add the tomato sauce, honey or maple syrup, and apple cider vinegar to the saucepan, and continue whisking until smooth and well combined.

7. Bring the enchilada sauce to a simmer over medium heat, then reduce the heat to low and let it simmer gently for 10-15 minutes, or until the sauce has thickened to your desired consistency

8. Once simmered, remove the saucepan from the heat and let the enchilada sauce cool for a few minutes.

9. Once cooled, transfer the enchilada sauce to an airtight container or jar.

10. Store the homemade enchilada sauce in the refrigerator for up to 1 week, or freeze for up to 3 months.

11. Use the homemade enchilada sauce as a flavorful and versatile ingredient in your Eosinophilic Esophagitis (EOE) diet, such as in enchiladas, tacos, burritos, or as a marinade for meats or tofu.

Enjoy this rich and flavorful homemade enchilada sauce as a delicious and nutritious addition to your Eosinophilic

Esophagitis (EOE) diet. Adjust the spiciness and seasoning according to your taste preferences, and feel free to customize the recipe with additional ingredients like diced onions, bell peppers, or jalapenos.

# CONCLUSION

Dear Reader, as you close the pages of this EOE Diet Cookbook, we hope you feel empowered and inspired to embark on a journey towards better health and well-being. Eosinophilic Esophagitis (EOE) and other food allergies present unique challenges, but with the right tools and knowledge, you can navigate them with confidence.

Throughout this book, we've delved into the intricacies of the Six Food Elimination Diet (6FED), providing you with a variety of gluten-free, dairy-free, egg-free, fish-free, soy-free, and nut-free recipes that cater to your dietary needs. From appetizers to beverages, we've covered all the bases, ensuring that every meal you prepare is not only safe but also delicious and satisfying. We've also shared valuable insights on ingredient substitutes, food groups, allergens, and labels, giving you a deeper understanding of how to make informed choices when it comes to your diet. And let's not forget our range of kitchen staples and condiments, which add flavor and variety to your meals while keeping allergens at bay. But beyond the recipes and dietary tips, this book is about more than just food. It's about embracing a lifestyle that prioritizes your health and well-being. It's about finding joy in the kitchen, even when faced with dietary restrictions. It's about feeling confident and empowered to make choices that support your body and mind.

As you embark on this journey, we encourage you to experiment, to get creative, and to make these recipes your own. And remember, this book is just the beginning. There are countless possibilities waiting to be discovered, and we hope you'll continue to explore and enjoy them.

Thank you for choosing this EOE Diet Cookbook. We hope it brings you joy, comfort, and delicious meals that nourish both your body and your soul. And if you've enjoyed this book, we kindly ask that you leave a positive review, so others can discover the benefits of the Six Food Elimination Diet and the joy of allergen-free cooking. I wish you health, happiness, and many delicious meals ahead.

# BONUS

Here are 4 bonuses for you;

## Bonus One; A Community for EOE Patients

This community is a community where you can join and gain access to over 1700 nutrient dense member only recipes and easy meal planning tools. For more information, visit the site below;

https://nourishingmeals.com/signup

Note that terms and conditions apply.

## Bonus Two: Esophageal Soft Diet Foods

When dealing with Eosinophilic Esophagitis (EOE) or any other condition that affects your esophagus, it's essential to focus on foods that are gentle on your digestive system. An esophageal soft diet consists of foods that are easy to swallow, digest, and do not irritate the esophagus. Here's a comprehensive list of esophageal soft diet foods that you can incorporate into your meal plan:

**1. Cooked Grains:** Cooked grains such as rice, oats, quinoa, and barley are soft and easy to swallow. They provide essential nutrients like carbohydrates, fiber, and some vitamins and minerals.

**2. Soft Breads:** Opt for soft breads like white, whole wheat, or gluten-free bread. Toasting the bread can make it easier to chew and swallow.

**3. Smooth Nut Butters:** Nut butters like almond butter, cashew butter, or peanut butter (if tolerated) are soft and easy to swallow. Ensure they are free of large pieces that can cause choking.

**4. Soft Fruits:** Choose soft fruits like bananas, avocados, ripe peaches, pears, and cooked apples. These fruits are not only easy to swallow but also provide vitamins, minerals, and fiber.

**5. Soft Vegetables:** Cooked vegetables like carrots, squash, sweet potatoes, and green beans are soft and easy to chew. Avoid raw or crunchy vegetables.

**6. Soft Proteins:** Opt for soft proteins like eggs, tofu, fish, chicken, or turkey. Avoid tough meats or meats with bones that can cause choking.

**7. Dairy Products:** Soft dairy products like yogurt, pudding, and cottage cheese are easy to swallow and provide essential nutrients like calcium and protein.

**8. Soups and Broths:** Soups and broths made with soft vegetables, grains, and proteins are easy to swallow and provide hydration and nutrients.

**9. Soft Desserts:** Choose soft desserts like gelatin, pudding, custard, or soft cookies. Avoid hard candies or desserts with nuts or large pieces that can cause choking.

**10. Beverages:** Opt for soft beverages like water, fruit juices, herbal teas, or smoothies. Avoid carbonated or caffeinated beverages.

**11. Soft Snacks:** Choose soft snacks like applesauce, fruit cups, or soft granola bars. Avoid hard or crunchy snacks.

Remember to chew your food thoroughly and eat slowly to reduce the risk of choking. It's also essential to stay hydrated by drinking plenty of fluids throughout the day. As always, consult with your healthcare provider or a registered dietitian before making significant changes to your diet. They can provide personalized guidance based on your specific needs and condition.

By incorporating these esophageal soft diet foods into your meal plan, you can ensure that you're providing your body with the necessary nutrients while being gentle on your esophagus. Enjoy your meals and make sure you take care of yourself!

# Bonus Three: A 14 Day EOE Diet Meal Plan

A 14-Day Eosinophilic Esophagitis (EOE) Meal Plan

## Day 1:

- **Breakfast:** Citrus-Ginger Immunity Shots

- **Lunch:** Moroccan Ground Recipes Kebobs served with Italian Red Cabbage Salad

- **Dinner:** Thai Coconut Vegetable Soup

- **Snack:** Strawberry-Chai Fruit Salad

## Day 2:

- Breakfast: Blueberry Cabbage Detox Smoothie

- Lunch: Mediterranean Vegetable Stew

- Dinner: Pulled Pork Lettuce Tacos

- Snack: Celery-Ginger Juice

## Day 3:

- **Breakfast:** Blueberry Kale Protein Smoothie

- **Lunch:** Japanese Cucumber Salad served with Brown Rice and Mushroom Pilaf

- **Dinner:** Baked Butter Beans with Basil and Garlic

- **Snack:** Honeydew-Cucumber Slushies


## Day 4:

- **Breakfast:** Pineapple-Cucumber-Mint Smoothie

- **Lunch:** Cabbage and Fennel Slaw served with Roasted Red Pepper Hummus

- **Dinner:** Smashed Potatoes

- **Snack:** Icy Matcha-Banana Smoothie


## Day 5:

- **Breakfast:** Citrus Green Smoothie

- **Lunch:** Romanesco Tabouli

- **Dinner:** Bacon Wrapped Chicken Meatballs served with Moroccan Ground Recipes Kebobs

- **Snack:** Pineapple Mint Smoothie


## Day 6:

- **Breakfast:** Refreshing Raspberry Ginger Smoothie

- **Lunch:** Pico Dc Gauo served with Mexican Pink Beans and Rice

- **Dinner:** Roasted Cherry Tomatoes

- **Snack:** Cranberry Ginger Mocktail


## Day 7:

- **Breakfast:** Citrus-Ginger Immunity Shots

- **Lunch:** Spring Green Detox Soup

- **Dinner:** Herbed Hummus

- **Snack:** Honeydew-Cucumber Slushies


## Day 8:

- **Breakfast:** Icy Matcha-Banana Smoothie

- **Lunch:** Thai Coconut Vegetable Soup

- **Dinner:** Baked Garlic Ginger Wings

- **Snack:** Celery-Ginger Juice


## Day 9:

- **Breakfast:** Blueberry Kale Protein Smoothie

- **Lunch:** Chickpea Dinner Rolls (Yeast Free-Grain Free Salad) served with Italian Red Cabbage Salad

- **Dinner:** Olive Tapenade

- **Snack:** Icy Matcha-Banana Smoothie

## Day 10:

- **Breakfast:** Blueberry Cabbage Detox Smoothie

- **Lunch:** Cabbage and Fennel Slaw served with Moroccan Ground Recipes Kebobs

- **Dinner:** Roasted Red Pepper Hummus

- **Snack:** Pineapple-Cucumber-Mint Smoothie

## Day 11:

- **Breakfast:** Citrus Green Smoothie

- **Lunch:** Romanesco Tabouli

- **Dinner:** Mexican Pink Beans and Rice

- **Snack:** Cranberry Ginger Mocktail

## Day 12:

- **Breakfast:** Refreshing Raspberry Ginger Smoothie

- **Lunch:** Spring Green Detox Soup

- **Dinner:** Moroccan Ground Recipes Kebobs served with Roasted Cherry Tomatoes

- **Snack:** Honeydew-Cucumber Slushies


## Day 13:

- **Breakfast:** Icy Matcha-Banana Smoothie

- **Lunch:** Thai Coconut Vegetable Soup

- **Dinner:** Olive Tapenade

- **Snack:** Celery-Ginger Juice


## Day 14:

- **Breakfast:** Blueberry Kale Protein Smoothie

- **Lunch:** Chickpea Dinner Rolls (Yeast Free-Grain Free Salad) served with Italian Red Cabbage Salad

- **Dinner:** Baked Garlic Ginger Wings

- **Snack:** Pineapple-Cucumber-Mint Smoothie

**Note:** This meal plan is a sample and can be adjusted based on individual preferences, dietary restrictions, and nutritional needs. Please consult with a healthcare provider or registered dietitian before making significant changes to your diet.

## Bonus Four: Diet Therapy for EOE

Eosinophilic Esophagitis (EOE) is a chronic allergic condition characterized by inflammation of the esophagus due to an allergic reaction to certain foods. While there is no cure for EOE, diet therapy plays a crucial role in managing symptoms and preventing flare-ups. Here's a comprehensive guide to diet therapy for EOE:

**1. Elimination Diet:** The first step in managing EOE is identifying and eliminating trigger foods from your diet. Common allergens that may trigger EOE include dairy, wheat, eggs, soy, nuts, and seafood. A healthcare provider or even a registered dietitian can help you to effectively create an elimination diet plan that would be tailored to your specific needs and wants.

**2. Six Food Elimination Diet (6FED):** The 6FED is a specific type of elimination diet that focuses on eliminating six major allergen groups: wheat, dairy, eggs, soy, nuts, and seafood. After eliminating these foods from your diet for a certain period, you'll gradually reintroduce them one at a time to determine which ones trigger your symptoms.

**3. Elemental Diet:** In some cases, a healthcare provider may recommend an elemental diet, which involves consuming only liquid nutrition formulas that contain predigested proteins and carbohydrates. This approach can provide relief for some individuals with EOE by eliminating potential allergens.

**4. Hypoallergenic Diet:** A hypoallergenic diet involves eliminating highly allergenic foods like dairy, wheat, eggs, soy, nuts, and seafood, as well as other potential allergens like corn, citrus fruits, and certain spices. This diet focuses on consuming foods that are less likely to trigger an allergic reaction.

**5. Anti-Inflammatory Diet:** An anti-inflammatory diet involves consuming foods that are rich in anti-inflammatory nutrients like omega-3 fatty acids, antioxidants, and fiber. This diet can help reduce inflammation in the esophagus and improve symptoms of EOE.

**6. Swallowing Techniques:** In addition to dietary changes, certain swallowing techniques can help manage symptoms of EOE. These techniques include chewing food thoroughly, eating slowly, and drinking plenty of fluids to help food pass through the esophagus more easily.

**7. Nutritional Supplements:** In some cases, nutritional supplements may be necessary to ensure you're getting adequate nutrients while following a restricted diet. These supplements may include vitamins, minerals, and protein powders.

**8. Food Allergy Testing:** Food allergy testing, such as skin prick tests or blood tests, can help identify specific foods that trigger allergic reactions in individuals with EOE. This information can guide dietary changes and help prevent future flare-ups.

**9. Regular Monitoring:** Once you've identified trigger foods and established a diet plan, it's essential to monitor your symptoms regularly. Keep a food diary to track your diet and symptoms, and make adjustments as needed to manage your EOE effectively.

**10. Consultation with Healthcare Providers:** It's crucial to work closely with a healthcare provider, such as a gastroenterologist, allergist, or registered dietitian, who has experience in managing EOE. They can provide guidance, support, and personalized recommendations to help you navigate the dietary challenges of EOE.

In conclusion, diet therapy plays a vital role in managing Eosinophilic Esophagitis (EOE). By identifying trigger foods, following an elimination diet, and making dietary adjustments, individuals with EOE can effectively manage symptoms and improve their quality of life. It's essential to work closely with healthcare providers to develop a personalized diet plan and monitor symptoms regularly. With proper dietary management, individuals with EOE can enjoy a healthy and fulfilling lifestyle.

# MEASUREMENTS AND CONVERSION TABLE

## 1. Volume Measurements:

- 1 teaspoon (tsp) = 5 milliliters (ml)

- 1 tablespoon (tbsp) = 15 milliliters (ml)

- 1 fluid ounce (fl oz) = 29.57 milliliters (ml)

- 1 cup = 240 milliliters (ml)

- 1 pint (16 fl oz) = 473 milliliters (ml)

- 1 quart (32 fl oz) = 946 milliliters (ml)

- 1 gallon (128 fl oz) = 3.785 liters (L)


## 2. Weight Measurements:

- 1 ounce (oz) = 28.35 grams (g)

- 1 pound (lb) = 16 ounces = 453.59 grams (g)

- 1 kilogram (kg) = 2.205 pounds (lbs)


## 3. Dry Ingredients:

- 1 cup all-purpose flour = 120 grams (g)

- 1 cup granulated sugar = 200 grams (g)

- 1 cup brown sugar = 220 grams (g)

- 1 cup powdered sugar = 125 grams (g)

- 1 cup rolled oats = 90 grams (g)

- 1 cup nuts (chopped) = 115 grams (g)

- 1 cup breadcrumbs = 100 grams (g)

## 4. Liquid Ingredients:

- 1 cup water = 240 milliliters (ml)

- 1 cup milk = 240 milliliters (ml)

- 1 cup buttermilk = 240 milliliters (ml)

- 1 cup vegetable oil = 240 milliliters (ml)

## 5. Temperature Conversions:

- 350°F = 175°C (moderate oven)

- 375°F = 190°C (moderately hot oven)

- 400°F = 200°C (hot oven)

- 425°F = 220°C (very hot oven)

## 6. Miscellaneous Conversions:

- 1 stick of butter = 1/2 cup = 113 grams (g)

- 1 clove of garlic = approximately 1/2 teaspoon minced

- 1 medium-sized onion = approximately 1 cup chopped

- 1 lemon = approximately 2-3 tablespoons of juice